THE PENGUIN BOOK OF
SOUTH AFRICAN VERSE

COMPILED AND INTRODUCED BY

JACK COPE AND UYS KRIGE

PENGUIN BOOKS

Penguin Books Ltd, Harmondsworth, Middlesex, England
Penguin Books Inc., 7110 Ambassador Road, Baltimore, Maryland 21207 U.S.A
Penguin Books Australia Ltd, Ringwood, Victoria, Australia

—

First published 1968
This anthology copyright © Uys Krige and Jack Cope 1968

—

Made and printed in Great Britain
by Cox & Wyman Ltd,
London, Reading and Fakenham
Set in Monotype Imprint

CONTENTS

CONTENTS

7

CONTENTS

9

CONTENTS

AFRICAN SECTION

1. *Bushman*

2. *Hottentot*

3. Sotho

4. Xhosa

CONTENTS

INTRODUCTION

Poetry is something of an obsession in South Africa, or perhaps it is a territory which for a variety of causes has always called from its often lonely inhabitants the response of song or verse-making. Certainly the earliest known peoples, Bushmen and Hottentots, were adepts at expressing their longings, their prayers and observations of life and nature in poetic forms of which unfortunately very few examples have been recorded. The Bantu migrants moving slowly into the area from Central Africa brought a well developed oral literature through which features of their historical past, their collective wisdom and folklore were preserved. They were active and warlike peoples who travelled light and, while they had largely shed such plastic arts as carving or the making of musical instruments, were pre-eminent as singers and dancers.

The white races moved in from the South over the last three centuries and for a long time of adjustment were content with the Bible and with what literary ties they were able to preserve to connect them with their origins in the Old World. But in succeeding generations they too became Africans; sun and land ate deep into their consciousness and the writers of another and colder hemisphere no longer filled their need. British settler writers began in the early decades of the nineteenth century to produce verse out of the South African experience, the most notable figure being Thomas Pringle, abolitionist and champion of Press freedom. He was a friend of Coleridge and derived from Burns and the English romantics. His compassionate involvement in the liberation and advancement of the less privileged peoples has continued for a century and a half to be an influence in the work of South African writers in English, not entirely to its advantage. It was only in recent times, and practically within a single generation, that this current of writing has been able to discard its missionary zeal, its external and therefore patronizing view and to turn towards a concrete and inward vision as an approach to a more integral and felt reality.

The development of Afrikaans into a separate and distinct language had taken place under the shadow of Dutch which remained until less than half a century ago officially the language used in church and state. War between the Boers and Britain gave to Afrikaans a vital impetus and it was in this language of the fireside that the first significant poets of the Afrikaner people expressed themselves in protest, defiance and consolation.

Beginning in effect only in the twentieth century, the growth of Afrikaans literature has been a remarkable achievement in which poetry has been and remains its highest point. The considerable body of poetry has in successive waves or movements over hardly six decades been enriched, deepened, nuanced. In Eugène Marais, Totius, Celliers, and Leipoldt the language found four authentic poetic voices, all of whom became articulate at the time of the people's deepest need and when the grammar and orthography had not yet been formulated.

The strongest influences at that time, as might have been expected, were nineteenth-century Dutch and English poetry. The next important departure came with the *Dertigers* (poets of the thirties) and with them the turn from a more generalized, romantic, and even 'national' approach towards the poetry of inner experience, of individualism and the search for identity. They brought a variety of influences among which the predominant ones were German and French symbolism – even an interest in the later Spanish poets such as Lorca. Foremost among this group were van Wyk Louw and Elisabeth Eybers, both of whom are still active. Opperman, the leading figure in the next decade, continued to use strict forms and a finely disciplined handling of material, and it was not until the late fifties that experimentation and the break-up of accepted forms began to be exploited with success.

The new generation of writers, loosely grouping themselves as the *Sestigers* (writers of the sixties) were responsible for significant developments in Afrikaans literature. Poets as well as fiction writers assimilated French, Spanish, English, American and other world influences into a far-reaching transformation of the local scene. Ingrid Jonker was the most gifted poet of this generation; she and others of her time added new dimensions to the use of the language. Like Peter Blum before him, Adam Small used a peculiar patois of 'coloured' Afrikaans mixed with English to achieve a pathos and irony under which burns the humiliated pride of the darker-skinned people of the Cape.

Pride in the Afrikaans language and its success in the production of a many-sided literature have helped place writers, and particularly poets, in a relatively advantageous position. The established poets are honoured national figures showered (though with some significant exceptions) with prizes and public awards; their poems are read on festive occasions and repeated in recitals on the state radio. Poets are commissioned to write plays and other works to celebrate important events and achievements. Large editions of new poems by well known writers sell out and go into reprints while publishers eagerly compete for manuscripts from young men and women who may have broken into print a few times in the literary journals. Anthologies of verse are popular and both schools and universities are alert to keep abreast of trends in poetry.

No satisfactory reflection of Afrikaans poetry as a whole can be given in this limited choice of translated poems. Many of the most famous poems in the language do not appear in our list. The poets introduced here cannot, of course, be adequately represented, while a number of excellent writers are not represented at all. The entire volume could well have been filled with original Afrikaans poems without any sacrifice in standards. Our selection is limited for a variety of causes; one being the restriction of space. But the main reason is the insurmountable difficulty of translating success-fully a poem of strict form, in rhyme and metre, particularly where the poet has made use of resources and qualities intrinsic to his language and so incommunicable in any other.

Mallarmé has said that a poem is made not out of thoughts but out of words. One feels tempted to paraphrase him by saying a poem is made not even of words but of vowels and consonants; that it is the interplay of vowels and consonants which makes the music – and that by translation you have an entirely different set of sounds and the music is no more. . . .

So we have confined ourselves to such translations as in our opinion do not fall too far below the merit of the original and have a certain claim to exist as verse in their own right.

When dealing with our earliest poetry, the literally stone-age songs and recitals of the Bushmen and Hottentots, it is not possible to speak of any sense of continuity. Observations made a century and more ago by the ethnologists Bleek and Hahn have arrested out of time a few isolated records besides which there is not much of value and reliability. The Hotten-tot language has become extinct and the Bushman dialects still surviving in the Kalahari desert are changing under the impact of Bantu and European languages. The examples given here, shaped from phonetically recorded originals, in reality belong to an age of incantation or primitive magical belief in which the singer or reciter gains certain powers over nature or life by the act of repetition.

By contrast with these archaic click languages the vernacu-lars of the Bantu peoples are lively and adaptable and have already shown themselves capable of assimilating new words and structures as well as a range of modern conceptions. The spoken word in a Bantu language may be modified by a variation of the vowel into as many as ten tones while a sys-tem of concords within the sentence conveys an interrelation of sound and meaning. This gives the languages, even in everyday speech, a notably harmonious or musical quality pleasing to the trained ear, although it presents an obstacle to the process of change into the era of written literature and, in poetry, is highly resistant to any effort at translation. Working into the relatively low and time-flattened rhythms of English, one is keenly aware of how much is lost. A 'praise' poem for instance, chanted or declaimed in a crescendo of exultation, violence and speed, becomes the vehicle of a mass emotional experience extending beyond its immediate meaning which, owing to its archaic language and forgotten allusions, may be but dimly understood by many in the audience. A single word can contain a weight of meaning or imagery that cannot be brought across in a whole line – with footnotes!

In the African languages the transition from the spoken to the written form of poetry is still in active process. Early mission-educated writers used their talents to compose hymns, and the influence of the Bible and Hymn-book has been profound in the entire development of written African literature. Other writers attempted to adapt their tongue to the forms of a Wordsworth or Tennyson and produced hybrid pastorals strange to any ear. But skills have grown and the evolution of original African forms subject to outside influences has been successfully carried forward by such poets as Mqhayi in Xhosa, Vilakazi in Zulu and a growing band of Sotho poets. The Sotho language, although spoken over a large area of South Africa, has the distinction of being the national language of a now independent state and its development may be expected to vary somewhat from that of the other local languages. Sotho poetry is already notable for its emphasis on national themes deriving from the cultivation of a strong historical sense.

African poets still speak largely in collective and impersonal terms and songs may be found of true poetic value which are in fact group products composed by a wedding choir or a location musical band. The poem of total individualism or of alienation and despair is likely to come from the man who has strayed far from his people, perhaps into exile, and probably will be written in English, not in his home language.

As in the case of Afrikaans, the small selection of translations from the African languages presented here is not more than an introduction to a large store of otherwise inaccessible poetry. Our choice has, again, been arbitrary and largely influenced by the advice of our collaborators in the different languages and by the possibility of making adequate translations. In the case of some of the 'praise' poems, such as those of the Zulu kings, the treatment has been severely selective, a liberty which African experts consider justified. No two reciters will deliver the poems in the same order or sequence with the result that any single transcription appears like a jumble of dissociated images and historical tags. In these extracts images and sequences have been reassembled in a more comprehensible order.

And finally, returning to the section written originally in English, we again plead having made a personal choice, aimed at being representative but subject to the usual limitations. One is a limit of time – nearly a century of 'colonial' verse has been left out of consideration. The present collection begins with Roy Campbell (born 1902) and is thus confined to our own times. Campbell and Plomer started a totally new direction in South African English verse – their fierce criticism and rejection of established values set them on a course from which there was no turning back. Their talent raised them far above all previous achievements. They did not come with the philanthropist's special pleading but with the whiplash – their magazine was called *Voorslag* (the whiplash). They were, however, more than critics and iconoclasts and their achievement stands well in contemporary literature.

The next distinctive movement in South African poetry took place under the impetus of war. The agony of the Spanish Civil War followed by the Second World War had stirred a generation of young South Africans many of whom had lived and worked in Europe and now saw their own homeland with new and estranged eyes. Some found themselves in uniform, others rejected war altogether. They questioned the glib slogans of the times as they turned inside out the entire assumptions on which they had been raised. The search for new loyalties, for any meaning in the suffering and waste, for self-identity – this marked the verse of the time. Currey, Prince, Delius and Butler, Eglington and Macnab were among the war generation. They brought into South African poetry the ease of spoken language, the dialogue of the army canteen and the station platform. Going into the years of peace, their technical proficiency carried them over difficult periods of adaptation to reaction; bitterness was tempered with irony.

Uys Krige's and E. Planje's lively magazine *Vandag* (Today) gave many of the poets of the time their first appearance in print. With them the women poets, Ruth Miller, Adèle Naudé and Phyllis Haring were also publishing. A few little collections were printed by adventurous publishers but the opportunity to publish always remained severely limited. In London or New York, literary magazines occasionally printed South African poems.

The latest period has brought a greatly increased interest in poetry together with the emergence of new talents and a stronger trend towards the inner personal vision, principally in such a poet as Sydney Clouts. The magazine *Contrast* began in 1960 to provide a new outlet for poetry, followed a few years later by Guy Butler's broadsheet *New Coin*. These two publications, and the older Afrikaans quarterly *Standpunte*, have done much for South African literature in recent years and many poems in this volume first appeared in their pages. With the darkening of political horizons currents of seriousness or of dissociation spread further in South African writing. There has been little inclination towards experiment for its own sake. Men and women of all races write verse in English – Anglo-Saxons, Jews, Afrikaners, Africans, Coloureds, Indians – and the language as a medium has collected undertones of protest, perhaps not the grand theme in poetry but revealing at least a recognizable thread through one aspect of the country's poetic output.

Dissociation goes far among South African writers, leading many on the English-speaking side into exile, either voluntary or perforce. Among the poets, Campbell and Plomer left the country early and others who live abroad include Currey, Prince, Wright, Lerner, Clouts, Delius, Barry Higgs, Jean Lipkin and Driver. Among the Afrikaner poets, three of the most talented have taken their own lives and those who have chosen to leave the country include Elisabeth Eybers, Olga Kirsch, Peter Blum, Sheila Cussons and Barend Toerien.

As translators we have relied on the insight of trained language experts and the ear of fellow poets. These include Dr Dan Kunene, the Sotho linguist, Mr M. C. Mcanyangwa, lecturer in Bantu languages; poets Ruth Miller, Adèle Naudé, Guy Butler and Anthony Delius. Invaluable assistance and advice have indeed come from many sides in the preparation of this book and we thank sincerely all who have been associated with us for their practical help, their faith and patience.

J.C. and U.K.

ENGLISH

ROY CAMPBELL

THE THEOLOGY OF BONGWI, THE BABOON

This is the wisdom of the Ape
    Who yelps beneath the Moon –
'Tis God who made me in His shape
    He is a Great Baboon.
'Tis He who tilts the moon askew
    And fans the forest trees,
The heavens which are broad and blue
    Provide him his trapeze;
He swings with tail divinely bent
    Around those azure bars
And munches to his Soul's content
    The kernels of the stars;
And when I die, His loving care
    Will raise me from the sod
To learn the perfect Mischief there,
    The Nimbleness of God.

BUFFEL'S KOP

(*Olive Schreiner's Grave*)

In after times when strength or courage fail,
May I recall this lonely hour: the gloom
Moving one way: all heaven in the pale
Roaring: and high above the insulated tomb
An eagle anchored on full spread of sail
That from its wings let fall a silver plume.

ROUNDING THE CAPE

The low sun whitens on the flying squalls,
Against the cliffs the long grey surge is rolled
Where Adamastor from his marble halls
Threatens the sons of Lusus as of old.

Faint on the glare uptowers the dauntless form,
Into whose shade abysmal as we draw,
Down on our decks, from far above the storm,
Grin the stark ridges of his broken jaw.

Across his back, unheeded, we have broken
Whole forests: heedless of the blood we've spilled,
In thunder still his prophecies are spoken,
In silence, by the centuries, fulfilled.

Farewell, terrific shade! though I go free
Still of the powers of darkness art thou Lord:
I watch the phantom sinking in the sea
Of all that I have hated and adored.

The prow glides smoothly on through seas quiescent:
But where the last point sinks into the deep,
The land lies dark beneath the rising crescent,
And Night, the Negro, murmurs in his sleep.

TRISTAN DA CUNHA

To Robert Lyle

Snore in the foam: the night is vast and blind;
The blanket of the mist about your shoulders,
Sleep your old sleep of rock, snore in the wind,
Snore in the spray! the storm your slumber lulls,
His wings are folded on your nest of boulders
As on their eggs the grey wings of your gulls.

No more as when, so dark an age ago,
You hissed a giant cinder from the ocean,
Around your rocks you furl the shawling snow
Half sunk in your own darkness, vast and grim,
And round you on the deep with surly motion
Pivot your league-long shadow as you swim.

Why should you haunt me thus but that I know
My surly heart is in your own displayed,
Round whom such leagues in endless circuit flow,
Whose hours in such a gloomy compass run –
A dial with its league-long arm of shade
Slowly revolving to the moon and sun.

My pride has sunk, like your grey fissured crags,
By its own strength o'ertoppled and betrayed:
I, too, have burned the wind with fiery flags
Who now am but a roost for empty words,
An island of the sea whose only trade
Is in the voyage of its wandering birds.

Did you not, when your strength became your pyre
Deposed and tumbled from your flaming tower,
Awake in gloom from whence you sank in fire,
To find, Antaeus-like, more vastly grown,
A throne in your own darkness, and a power
Sheathed in the very coldness of your stone?

Your strength is that you have no hope or fear,
You march before the world without a crown,
The nations call you back, you do not hear,
The cities of the earth grow grey behind you,
You will be there when their great flames go down
And still the morning in the van will find you.

You march before the continents, you scout
In front of all the earth; alone you scale
The mast-head of the world, a lorn look-out
Waving the snowy flutter of your spray
And gazing back in infinite farewell
To suns that sink and shores that fade away.

From your grey tower what long regrets you fling
To where, along the low horizon burning,
The great swan-breasted seraphs soar and sing,
And suns go down, and trailing splendours dwindle,
And sails on lonely errands unreturning
Glow with a gold no sunrise can rekindle.

Turn to the night; these flames are not for you
Whose steeple for the thunder swings its bells;
Grey Memnon, to the tempest only true,
Turn to the night, turn to the shadowing foam,
And let your voice, the saddest of farewells,
With sullen curfew toll the grey wings home.

The wind, your mournful siren, haunts the gloom;
The rocks, spray-clouded, are your signal guns
Whose stony nitre, puffed with flying spume,
Rolls forth in grim salute your broadside hollow
Over the gorgeous burials of suns
To sound the tocsin of the storms that follow.

Plunge forward like a ship to battle hurled,
Slip the long cables of the failing light,
The level rays that moor you to the world:
Sheathed in your armour of eternal frost,
Plunge forward, in the thunder of the fight
To lose yourself as I would fain be lost.

Exiled like you and severed from my race
By the cold ocean of my own disdain,
Do I not freeze in such a wintry space,
Do I not travel through a storm as vast
And rise at times, victorious from the main,
To fly the sunrise at my shattered mast?

Your path is but a desert where you reap
Only the bitter knowledge of your soul:
You fish with nets of seaweed in the deep
As fruitlessly as I with nets of rhyme –
Yet forth you stride, yourself the way, the goal,
The surges are your strides, your path is time.

Hurled by what aim to what tremendous range!
A missile from the great sling of the past,
Your passage leaves its track of death and change
And ruin on the world: you fly beyond
Leaping the current of the ages vast
As lightly as a pebble skims a pond.

The years are undulations in your flight
Whose awful motion we can only guess –
Too swift for sense, too terrible for sight,
We only know how fast behind you darken
Our days like lonely beacons of distress:
We know that you stride on and will not harken.

Now in the eastern sky the fairest planet
Pierces the dying waves with dangled spear,
And in the whirring hollows of your granite
That vaster sea to which you are a shell
Sighs with a ghostly rumour, like the drear
Moan of the night wind in a hollow cell.

We shall not meet again; over the wave
Our ways divide, and yours is straight and endless,
But mine is short and crooked to the grave:
Yet what of these dark crowds amid whose flow
I battle like a rock, aloof and friendless,
Are not their generations vague and endless
The waves, the strides, the feet on which I go?

MASS AT DAWN

I dropped my sail and dried my dripping seines
Where the white quay is chequered by cool planes
In whose great branches, always out of sight,
The nightingales are singing day and night.
Though all was grey beneath the moon's grey beam,
My boat in her new paint shone like a bride,
And silver in my basket shone the bream:
My arms were tired and I was heavy-eyed,
But when with food and drink, at morning-light,
The children met me at the water-side,
Never was wine so red or bread so white.

HORSES ON THE CAMARGUE
To A. F. Tschiffely

In the grey wastes of dread,
The haunt of shattered gulls where nothing moves
But in a shroud of silence like the dead,
I heard a sudden harmony of hooves,
And, turning, saw afar
A hundred snowy horses unconfined,
The silver runaways of Neptune's car
Racing, spray-curled, like waves before the wind.
Sons of the Mistral, fleet
As him with whose strong gusts they love to flee,
Who shod the flying thunders on their feet

30

And plumed them with the snortings of the sea;
Theirs is no earthly breed
Who only haunt the verges of the earth
And only on the sea's salt herbage feed –
Surely the great white breakers gave them birth.
For when for years a slave,
A horse of the Camargue, in alien lands,
Should catch some far-off fragrance of the wave
Carried far inland from his native sands,
Many have told the tale
Of how in fury, foaming at the rein,
He hurls his rider; and with lifted tail,
With coal-red eyes and cataracting mane,
Heading his course for home,
Though sixty foreign leagues before him sweep,
Will never rest until he breathes the foam
And hears the native thunder of the deep.
But when the great gusts rise
And lash their anger on these arid coasts,
When the scared gulls career with mournful cries
And whirl across the waste like driven ghosts:
When hail and fire converge,
The only souls to which they strike no pain
Are the white-crested fillies of the surge
And the white horses of the windy plain.
Then in their strength and pride
The stallions of the wilderness rejoice;
They feel their Master's trident in their side,
And high and shrill they answer to his voice.
With white tails smoking free,
Long steaming manes, and arching necks, they show
Their kinship to their sisters of the sea –
And forward hurl their thunderbolts of snow.
Still out of hardship bred,
Spirits of power and beauty and delight
Have ever on such frugal pastures fed
And loved to course with tempests through the night.

CHOOSING A MAST

This mast, new-shaved, through whom I rive the ropes,
Says she was once an oread of the slopes,
Graceful and tall upon the rocky highlands,
A slender tree as vertical as noon,
And her low voice was lovely as the silence
Through which a fountain whistles to the moon,
Who now of the white spray must take the veil
And, for her songs, the thunder of the sail.

I chose her for her fragrance, when the spring
With sweetest resins swelled her fourteenth ring
And with live amber welded her young thews:
I chose her for the glory of the Muse,
Smoother of forms, that her hard-knotted grain,
Grazed by the chisel, shaven by the plane,
Might from the steel as cool a burnish take
As from the bladed moon a windless lake.

I chose her for her eagerness of flight
Where she stood tiptoe on the rocky height
Lifted by her own perfume to the sun,
While through her rustling plumes with eager sound
Her eagle spirit, with the gale at one,
Spreading wide pinions, would have spurned the ground
And her own sleeping shadow, had they not
With thymy fragrance charmed her to the spot.

Lover of song, I chose this mountain pine
Not only for the straightness of her spine
But for her songs: for there she loved to sing
Through a long noon's repose of wave and wing,
The fluvial swirling of her scented hair
Sole rill of song in all that windless air,
And her slim form the naiad of the stream
Afloat upon the languor of its theme;

And for the soldier's fare on which she fed:
Her wine the azure, and the snow her bread;
And for her stormy watches on the height,
For only out of solitude or strife
Are born the sons of valour and delight;
And lastly for her rich, exulting life,
That with the wind stopped not its singing breath
But carolled on, the louder for its death.

Under a pine, when summer days were deep,
We loved the most to lie in love or sleep:
And when in long hexameters the west
Rolled his grey surge, the forest for his lyre,
It was the pines that sang us to our rest,
Loud in the wind and fragrant in the fire,
With legioned voices swelling all night long,
From Pelion to Provence, their storm of song.

It was the pines that fanned us in the heat,
The pines, that cheered us in the time of sleet,
For which sweet gifts I set one dryad free;
No longer to the wind a rooted foe,
This nymph shall wander where she longs to be
And with the blue north wind arise and go,
A silver huntress with the moon to run
And fly through rainbows with the rising sun;

And when to pasture in the glittering shoals
The guardian mistral drives his thundering foals,
And when like Tartar horsemen racing free
We ride the snorting fillies of the sea,
My pine shall be the archer of the gale
While on the bending willow curves the sail
From whose great bow the long keel shooting home
Shall fly, the feathered arrow of the foam.

THE SECRET MUSE

Between the midnight and the morn,
To share my watches late and lonely,
There dawns a presence such as only
Of perfect silence can be born.
On the blank parchment falls the glow
Of more than daybreak: and one regal
Thought, like the shadow of an eagle,
Grazes the smoothness of its snow.
Though veiled to me that face of faces
And still that form eludes my art,
Yet all the gifts my faith has brought
Along the secret stair of thought
Have come to me on those hushed places
Whose footfall is my beating heart.

DRIVING CATTLE TO CASAS BUENAS

The roller perched upon the wire,
Telegrams running through his toes,
At my approach would not retire
But croaked a greeting as he rose,
A telegraph of solar fire.
Girth-high the poppies and the daisies
To brush the belly of my mule:
The thyme was smoking up God's praises.
The sun was warm, the wind was cool,
The white sierra was the icy
Refrigerator of that noon
And in the air so fresh, so spicy,
So steep, so pale, Toledo's June,
The sun seemed smaller than the moon.
Wading through seas of fire and blood
(I never saw such flowers before)
I said to Apis, 'What a cud

To make the bulls of Bashan roar!'
The church, with storks upon the steeple,
And scarcely could my cross be signed,
When round me came those Christian people
So hospitably clean, and kind.
Beans and Alfalfa in the manger –
Alfalfa, there was never such!
And rice and rabbit for the stranger.
Thank you very much!

LUIS DE CAMÕES

Camões, alone, of all the lyric race,
Born in the black aurora of disaster,
Can look a common soldier in the face:
I find a comrade where I sought a master:
For daily, while the stinking crocodiles
Glide from the mangroves on the swampy shore,
He shares my awning on the dhow, he smiles,
And tells me that he lived it all before.
Through fire and shipwreck, pestilence and loss,
Led by the ignis fatuus of duty
To a dog's death – yet of his sorrows king –
He shouldered high his voluntary Cross,
Wrestled his hardships into forms of beauty,
And taught his gorgon destinies to sing.

BALLAD OF DON JUAN TENORIO
AND THE STATUE OF THE COMENDADOR

Ten cuckolds slain without confession
In duels, by the waterfront
Of Hades, in glum procession
Are singing out for Charon's punt.

Ten weeping women dry their clothes
Washed up along the homeless sands
By the red sea of perjured oaths
That shoals with amputated hands.

These were the fruits of all your swagger!
But through their tears will swim no more
Those ice-cold fish, your sword and dagger,
Whose fin-wake is a streak of gore;

For now the hour is aiming at you,
Tenorio! with its finger hooked:
Remember when you cuffed the statue
Upon the grave: and how it looked:

And how it seemed to nod its head
When you invited it to dine.
If you were wise to tempt the dead
You verify tonight, at nine.

The stars are like cicadas chirping
With cold: but it is snug in here,
The throne of opulence usurping,
Beneath this costly chandelier.

The firelight twinkles on the jewels
Of pistol-butts: the rays enthrall
The glinting cutlery of duels
That hang for trophies round the wall.

Your Rolls sleeps safely in its garage,
Your Derby-winner in his stall:
But with a prayer balloon your barrage
Against the doom that's due to fall.

Pay off your cook and sack your butler:
Renounce your sacrilegious vow:
Though Satan were Toledo's cutler
No swordplay could avail you now.

A sentence Lawyers cannot garble
Has just been read: the tombs are still:
But from their garrisons of marble
One headstone moves along the hill.

The wind begins to grow much colder,
The grass with icicles to clink:
To pedestal the skating boulder
Each rivulet becomes a rink.

The river bridged itself with crystal
To its refrigerating tread,
The moon rose masked, and cocked the pistol
Of silence to the world's bald head.

Its passing starched the breath of bulls
Along the Guadalquivir's shore,
And froze the ferryman who pulls
More at his wineskin than his oar.

It seems your hounds have scented trouble.
The room grows arctic: moments drag:
Tenorio! pour yourself a double
To entertain the stalking crag.

Tenorio! it's too late for banter,
The statue knocks; the door gives way;
The whiskey froze in the decanter
And has not melted to this day.

One handshake: then the detonation:
A stench of nitre fills the hall:
The Butler on investigation
Retrieved one tiepin: that was all.

Out to the tombs the Civil Guard
Followed the clues of all they heard.
But though one hand seemed slightly charred,
The statue would not speak one word.

FISHING BOATS IN MARTIGUES

Around the quays, kicked off in twos
The Four Winds dry their wooden shoes.

UPON A GLOOMY NIGHT
St John of the Cross
Translation by Roy Campbell

Upon a gloomy night
With all my cares to loving ardours flushed,
(O venture of delight!)
With nobody in sight
I went abroad when all my house was hushed.

In safety, in disguise,
In darkness up the secret stair I crept,
(O happy enterprise)
Concealed from other eyes
When all my house at length in silence slept.

Upon that lucky night
In secrecy, inscrutable to sight,
I went without discerning
And with no other light
Except for that which in my heart was burning.

It lit and led me through
More certain than the light of noonday clear
To where One waited near
Whose presence well I knew,
There where no other presence might appear.

Oh night that was my guide!
Oh darkness dearer than the morning's pride,
Oh night that joined the lover
To the beloved bride
Transfiguring them each into the other.

Within my flowering breast
Which only for himself I save
He sank into his rest
And all my gifts I gave
Lulled by the airs with which the cedars wave.

Over the ramparts fanned
While the fresh wind was fluttering his tresses,
With his serenest hand
My neck he wounded, and
Suspended every sense with its caresses.

Lost to myself I stayed
My face upon my lover having laid
From all endeavour ceasing:
And all my cares releasing
Threw them amongst the lilies there to fade.

WILLIAM PLOMER

THE PRISONER

Every morning the prisoner hears
Calls to action and words of warning:
They fall not on deaf but indifferent ears.

Free speech, fresh air are denied him now,
Are not for one who is growing thin
Between four walls of Roman thickness.
From his cell he sees the meetings begin,
The vehement look on the orator's brow
And the listeners warped by want and sickness.

His old wound throbs as old wounds will,
The summer morning makes his head feel light,
Painful the sunlight on the whitewashed sill,
Trembling he awaits the ever-fruitful night,
For then dreams many-formed appear
Teeming with truths that public lips ignore,
And naked figures struggle from the sea
Shipwrecked, to be clothed on shore,
And words no orator utters are said
Such as the wind through mouths of ivy forms
Or snails with silver write upon the dead
Bark of an ilex after April storms.

While flights of bombers streak his patch of sky,
While speakers rant and save the world with books,
While at the front the first battalions die,
Over the edge of thought itself he looks,
Tiptoe along a knife-edge he slowly travels,
Hears the storm roaring, the serpent hiss,
And the frail rope he hangs by, twisting, unravels,
As he steps so lightly over the abyss.

THE DEVIL-DANCERS

In shantung suits we whites are cool,
Glasses and helmets censoring the glare;
Fever has made our anxious faces pale,
We stoop a little from the load we bear;

Grouped in the shadow of the compound wall
We get our cameras ready, sitting pensive;
Keeping our distance and our dignity
We talk and smile, though slightly apprehensive.

The heat strikes upward from the ground,
The ground the natives harden with their feet,
The flag is drooping on its bamboo pole,
The middle distance wavers in the heat.

Naked or gaudy, all agog the crowd
Buzzes and glistens in the sun; the sight
Dazzles the retina; we remark the smell,
The drums beginning, and the vibrant light.

Now the edge of the jungle rustles. In a hush
The crowd parts. Nothing happens. Then
The dancers stalk adroitly out on stilts,
Weirdly advancing, twice as high as men.

Sure as fate, strange as the mantis, cruel
As vengeance in a dream, four bodies hung
In cloaks of rasping grasses, turning
Their tiny heads, the masks besmeared with dung;

Each mops and mows, uttering no sound,
Each stately, awkward, giant marionette,
Each printed shadow frightful on the ground
Moving in small distorted silhouette;

The fretful pipes and thinly-crying strings,
The mounting expectation of the drums
Excite the nerves, and stretch the muscles taut
Against the climax – but it never comes;

It never comes because the dance must end
And soon the older dancers will be dead;
We leave by air tomorrow. How
Can ever these messages by us be read?

These bodies hung with viscera and horns
Move with an incomparable lightness,
And through the masks that run with bullocks' blood
Quick eyes aim out, dots of fanatic brightness.

Within the mask the face, and moulded
(As mask to face) within the face the ghost,
As in its chrysalis-case the foetus folded
Of leaf-light butterfly. What matters most

When it comes out and we admire its wings
Is to remember where its life began:
Let us take care – that flake of flame may be
A butterfly whose bite can kill a man.

BLIND SAMSON

Their mockery brought him double force,
They gave him (ruined by their gain)
Clear sight to see his destiny
And make their smallness plain.

The smallness of the seeming great
Taught him to make no compromise,
His anger smashed their mocking skulls
And stopped their grinning eyes.

FATHER AND SON:
1939

A family portrait not too stale to record
Of a pleasant old buffer, nephew to a lord,
Who believed that the bank was mightier than the sword,
And that an umbrella might pacify barbarians abroad:
   Just like an old liberal
   Between the wars.

With an easy existence, and a cosy country place,
And with hardly a wrinkle, at sixty, in his face,
Growing old with old books, with old wine, and with grace,
Unaware that events move at a breakneck pace:
   Just like an old diehard
   Between the wars.

With innocuous tastes in common with his mate,
A love of his garden and his tidy snug estate,
Of dogs, music and children, and lying in bed late,
And no disposition to quarrel with his fate:
   Just like an old Englishman
   Between the wars.

With no religion or imagination, and a hazy lazy view
Of the great world where trouble kept cropping up anew,
With old clubmen for friends, who would seem stuffy to you,
Old faded prigs, but gentlemen (give them their due):
   Just like an old fossil
   Between the wars.

With a kindly old wife who subscribed for the oppressed,
With an O.B.E., and hair-do like a last year's bird's nest,
Even more tolerant than anyone would have guessed,
Who hoped that in the long run all was for the best:
   Just like an old lady
   Between the wars.

With one child, a son, who in spite of his education
Showed only a modicum of common sense or cultivation,
Sometimes read the *Daily Worker* or the *New Statesman and
       Nation*,
But neither, it must be admitted, with much concentration:
      Just like a young playboy
      Between the wars.

With a firm grasp of half-truths, with political short-sight
With a belief we could disarm but at the same time fight,
And that only the Left Wing could ever be right,
And that Moscow, of all places, was the sole source of light:
      Just like a young hopeful
      Between the wars.

With a flash flat in Chelsea of a bogus elegance,
With surrealist pictures and books puffed by Gollancz,
With a degree of complacence which nothing could enhance,
And without one sole well-wisher to kick him in the pants:
      Just like a young smarty
      Between the wars.

With a precious mistress who thought she could paint
But could neither show respect nor exercise restraint,
Was a perfect goose-cap, and thought good manners quaint,
With affectation enough to try the patience of a saint:
      Just like a young cutie
      Between the wars.

With a succession of parties for sponges and bores,
With a traffic-jam outside (for they turned up in scores),
With first-rate sherry flowing into second-rate whores,
And third-rate conversation without one single pause:
      Just like a young couple
      Between the wars.

With week-ends in the country and holidays in France,
With promiscuous habits, time to sunbathe and dance,
And even to write books that were hardly worth a glance,
Earning neither reputation nor the publisher's advance:
        Just like a young writer
        Between the wars.

On a Sunday in September other troubles had begun,
There was argument at lunch between the father and the son,
Smoke rose from Warsaw and the beef was underdone,
Nothing points to heaven now but the anti-aircraft gun:
        With a hey nonny nonny
        And a hi-de-ho.

Oh, the 'twenties and the 'thirties were not otherwise designed
Than other times when blind men into ditches led the blind,
When the rich mouse ate the cheese and the poor mouse got
        the rind,
And man, the self-destroyer, was not lucid in his mind:
        With a hey nonny nonny
        And a hi-de-ho.

BAMBOO

A Ballad for two voices

I

SHE: However dry and windless
        Cold days, hot nights may be,
        Bamboo, incessant rustler,
        Your restless leafage utters
        A sound of wind and rain:
        Nobody knows the nervous
        Effect it has on me –
        I cannot stand the strain,
        Bamboo, I cannot stand it,
        Your whispering campaign!

45

HE:
I love, bamboo, your fidgets
And sudden sighs, bamboo;
Awake alone I listen
To secret susurration
Like paper scraping stone;
Stroking the inner surface
Of this old heart, bamboo,
Whisper to me alone
Your wordless reminiscence –
And resurrect my own!

SHE:
Here is the explanation
Why what he loves I hate:
My husband was a sailor
Out on the China Station –
(If I had known him then!
It seems the best life offers
Is second-best and late;
Unsure of *what* and *when*
A girl may miss her chances –
What did I know of men?)

The girl he'll never talk of
And never can forget
Has always come between us:
I see her sly and slant-eyed
Haunting some furtive wood,
Slender in silk, and artful;
The moment that they met
Her doubtful maidenhood
Pleased him beyond all reason –
She stole his heart for good.

Before I ever knew him
The dew, the down, the bloom
Were brushed away in Asia –
Hers was his startling April,
His wildfire blossoming.
The years of humdrum fondness,
The habit-forming room
Are quite another thing –
I hate her for devouring
His unrecurring spring!

HE: Her skin was like a primrose,
In sheets of silk her feet
Slender as sleeping finches
Slept while the snow was heaping
A feather barricade
Between us and the future:
At first, so sly and sweet,
It seemed an escapade,
But we were caught together –
Love caught us while we played.

I felt her small heart racing,
Quick heart imprisoned in
Her flexile, bird-boned body,
As if another being
Conscious that it was mute
Beat desperate, beat lonely,
Against the screen of skin:
The hot moon smelt of fruit,
Looming up huge to listen
To one thin bamboo flute.

And that is why I planted
A thicket of bamboo
Here in an English garden –
Waving bamboo was witness
Of all that love can be:
I live at home and listen,
And you revive, bamboo,
After a life at sea,
The only overwhelming
Love ever shown to me.

SHE: How I dislike the supple
Canes, and the harsh coarse leaves!
There's something so suburban
About bamboos.

HE: The waving
Bamboo recalls the sway
Of young and fertile bodies
And lifted, long, silk sleeves.

SHE: Suburban, as I say.

HE: The wordless reminiscence
Is whispered night and day.

2

SHE: Now that he's dead and buried
At last, at last I'm free
To make my chosen changes
Put off when he was living:
I'm captain now, and crew –
(No freedom like a widow's!) –
And who's to disagree
With what I mean to do?
Root, shoot, and stem and sucker,
I'll root out that bamboo!

HIS GHOST: (*softly, from a distance*)
That's what you think, old helpmate,
But always I shall swim
Along your psyche's courses,
The frogman in your bloodstream
You never can evade;
By cutting down that sappy
Bamboo you'd injure him
Whose peace of mind you made –
You know you'll never touch it
With secateurs or spade!

3

HIS GHOST: Bamboo, she used to hate you
But lonely now she hears
And half believes your voice is
Not yours but mine – ironic
That she discovers now
A soft association,
Even a source of tears,
In what she once described as
'A vicious rasping sound' –
It now puts her in mind of
Her husband underground.

SHE: Strange, that I used to hate you,
His keepsake plant, bamboo!
In solitude your sighings
Recall my old companion
And not his dreamt-of past.

HIS GHOST: We phantoms have our triumphs.

SHE: You're *my* plant now, bamboo!

HIS GHOST: She understands at last
Why I was pleased to hear you.

SHE: I understand at last.

HIS GHOST: Hush-hush those open secrets
            You'll much rehearse alone
            When we are both reduced to
            Potential fertilizer
            For plants like you, bamboo.

SHE: Two butterflies beside you
            A moment on a stone –

HE: Would not be us, bamboo!
            And now long life we wish you,
            Long-loved, light-leaved bamboo.

HIS GHOST: *(together, very softly)*
SHE: Bamboo, bamboo, bamboo!

ALAN PATON

I HAVE APPROACHED

I have approached a moment of sterility
I shall not write any more awhile
For there is nothing more meretricious
Than to play with words.
Yet they are all there within me
The great living host of them
The gentle, the compassionate
The bitter and the scornful
The solemn and the sorrowful
The words of the childhood that will not come again.
But they do not come out for nothing
They do not form themselves into meanings
Unless some price has been paid for them
Unless some deep thing is felt that runs
Like a living flame through their shapes and forms
So that they catch fire and fuse themselves
Into glowing incandescences
Or if the felt thing is deep indeed,
Into conflagrations, so that the pen
Smokes in the hand, and the hand
Burns to the bone, and the paper chars
Under the heat of composition.
Therefore words, stay where you are awhile
Till I am able to call you out,
Till I am able to call you with authentic voice
So that the great living host of you
Tumble out and form immediately
Into parties, commandos, and battalions
Briefly saluting and wheeling away instantly
To waken the sleeping consciences
To call back to duty the absenting obligations
To assault again, night and day, month and year
The fortresses and bastions of our fears.

THE PRISON HOUSE

I ran from the prison house but they captured me
And he met me there at the door with a face of doom
And motioned me to go to his private room
And he took my rank from me, and gave me the hell
Of his tongue, and ordered me to the runaway cell
With the chains and the walls, and the long night days, and
    the gloom.

And once on leave that goes to the well-behaved
I jumped in fright from the very brothel bed
And through the midnight streets like a mad thing fled
Sobbing with fear lest the door be closed on me
And in silence he let me pass, he let me be,
No word but your clothing's disarranged, he said.

And once in a place where I was, I told a man
Whence I was come, and who was in charge, and he
Said God, but I never thought in my life to see
A man from that place, and I wish to God I was there,
Yes. I wish I was there. So I went back on air
And he smiled at me at the door, he smiled at me.

And once when he drew the blood from my rebel flesh
With foul and magnificent words I cursed and reviled
His name and his house and his works, and drunk with my
    pain and wild
I seized the whip from his hands and slashed him again
And again and again, and made him pay for my pain,
And I fell at his feet and wept on the stone like a child.

He can take the hide from my back, the sight from my eyes
The lust of my loins and the sounds of the earth from me,
Fruit's taste, and the scent of the flowers and the salt of the
    sea,
The thoughts of the mind, and the words of music and fire
That comforted me, so long as he does not require
These chains that now are become as garments to me.

HERMAN CHARLES BOSMAN

SEED

The farmer ploughs into the ground
More than the wheat-seed strewn on the ground.
The farmer ploughs into the ground
The plough and the oxen and his body.
He ploughs into the ground the farmstead and the cattle
And the pigs and the poultry and the kitchen utensils
And the afternoon sunlight shining into the window of the
    voorhuis
And the light entangled in the eyes of his children.
He ploughs into the ground his wife's brown body
And the windmill above the borehole
And the borehole and the wind driving the windmill
The farmer ploughs the blue clouds into the ground.
And as a tribute to the holocaust of the ploughshare
– To the sowing that was the parting of the Juggernaut –
The earth renders the farmer in due season
Corn.

LEARNING DESTINY

One last look at your hills, Lysander,
With the purple of grapes
And of blood and the undermost waves of the sea;
There was only one story
That was so honey-filled with glory,
So gangway-full of murders, laughters, rapes –
And I, with the restraint on me
Of the Christian's God, was a bystander
When a new world was born
In the reaping of yellow corn,
And the treading down of green corn.

OLD I AM

Old am I in years and Wisdom and
In nought else. Wave a wand
And, lo, I strive
To bring alive
Any old cause that's lost.
I am there at Zama with Hannibal's host;
With Rupert of the Rhine
At Naseby village; in the Confederate line
At whatever the South's last battle was.
Name but a defeated cause,
Prince Charlie at Culloden, then
Count me with those vanquished men
Who with targe and claymore will never take the high-road
     to Loch Lomond again.

I am old in years and in all things save
My veneration for the grave
In field or fen
Of one who fell flagless, unsung,
On a lost field and slept among
His neighbour men.

R. N. CURREY

COCK-CROW

This sudden cockerel who stood
Across the smoke-gold dawn and crowed
Became the bird who hid the sun
Crowing in morning Babylon;
The Talmud cock whose brazen plumes
Curved fanwise up the beaten roof
Of heaven in shadowed bas-relief,
Out-stretching fire-scalloped tips
To east and west in the eclipse;
His spurred feet on the earth; his comb
Touching the Zenith; his huge voice
Making the heart of God rejoice.

ULTIMATE EXILE IV

Is this the ultimate exile no man born
Can find return from, save for moments only,
By which each living man must wander lonely
From the convulsive moment when he's torn
Helpless into the light; and every dawn
Turn blinking from the glare towards some kindly
Dream of enfolding darkness, of the only
And multifoliate rose without a thorn?

The more a man's alive the more this steady
Search for the heart of darkness, and his time
Is given to this one thing and this thing only:
How to leave light of day behind, and climb
Onto the darkness of a woman's body,
Whence to be born again, helpless and lonely.

SONG

There is no joy in water apart from the sun,
There is no beauty not emphasized by death,
No meaning in home if exile were unknown;
A man who lives in a thermostat lives beneath
A bell of glass alone with the smell of death.

There is no beauty like that seen from a cliff;
The beauty of women comes and goes with a breath;
A man must offer the beauty of his wife
In sacrifice to give his children breath –
The children will walk on their folded hands of death.

Nothing in life is near and nothing far
Apart from love; a man can live beneath
His roof more lonely than an outer star;
And know a woman's beauty, a flower's breath
Walking alone in the valley of the shadow of death.

CHILDREN WAKING:
INDIAN HILL STATION

Like birds when first light breaks,
One of them stirs, and speaks;
The other drowsily
Makes some reply.

I cannot where I lie
Make out their commentary,
But chuckling word on word
Tells their accord;

Their brittle flow of words
Echoes the chirp of birds;
Without proviso they
Accept the day;

While their half-chant has thrown
My thoughts back to my own
Two boys who laugh and play
War years away;

Whose morning orisons
Used to awake me once,
Prelude to culmination
In invasion –

Their barefoot blitzkrieg! We
Were buried helplessly
Beneath the rosy flood
Of flesh and blood.

This one dive-bombed the sheet,
The other mined our feet,
While both drove clutching tanks
Across our flanks.

Checked at this point, they
Might for a moment stay
Quiet beneath some stale
Time-serving tale;

But their bridgehead was won
And our resistance done;
We must accept, as they
The fact of a new day.

IN MEMORIAM: ROY CAMPBELL

He grew where waves ride nine feet high
Like Zulu impis on the beach
Crested with sound, and every boy
Must watch for the whites-of-eyes of each.

Long rollers horned like bulls, would gore
Into the whinnying groins of sand,
And every boy, a matador
Must hold his courage out, and stand.

He learned to watch the rush and lunge,
And feel his feet, and wait until
The moment came for him to plunge
Into the envy poised to kill;

To plunge, and come through to a world
Of triumph on the other side,
When he is lifted up and whirled
Down the long combers of his pride.

MARRAKECH

Joseph Ben Tachfin came from the Sahara
With Potiphar's wife and army, crossed the plain
With a desert Arab's sensitive nose for water,
And an eye that saw the whole long way to Spain.

He brought his restlessness to Marrakech
Across the desert, over the High Atlas,
Then cut these wells and conduits for the fresh
Water to float this lily, this oasis.

This scatter of dark-leaved tents, these walls of ochre,
This quivering frieze of white-pavilioned mountains,
These date-palms of a desert tribe's nostalgia,
The princely palaces, the private fountains,

And the great public square, that unkempt garden
That glows at dusk with men who breathe out fire,
Weave necklaces of snakes, or spells to harden
Our hearts to courage, bodies to desire;

Floating on water, held in air like glass,
Bright in the glitter of the untouched snow –
The restlessness that thrust across the pass
Made this a stage, with further yet to go;

For, lily out of lily, against the sunset,
Grows the Koutoubia, imperial tower;
It looks to the Giralda in Seville, and Rabat,
Backwards and forwards to the Muslim hour.

HALO

Pastor M'Gadi's startling blackness
In my father's study, taking tea,
His smile for me as white as the saucer
Balanced like privilege on his knee.

Pastor M'Gadi in the drab location
Reading his letter by his gap of door;
Waiting by my horse, I watched his pigeons
White as the paper from my father's drawer.

Pastor M'Gadi's brilliant blackness
Laughing in the sun by his pigeon-cote,
Wearing a fluttering halo of fantails
White as the celluloid about his throat.

REMEMBERING SNOW

Today I think of a boy in the Transvaal
Spending his Christmas Day at the krantzes
Where the khaki drought of veld, cleft open,
Held festivals of water in a fern-green canyon.

We dived fork-naked into crystal pools,
Explored behind the maidenhair waterfalls,
Eating our Christmas pudding beneath the grace
Of feminine willows on the vivid grass.

My mother lured the pony with lumps of sugar;
We coaxed him into his creaking cat's cradle of leather,
My father, all that tawny homeward run,
Remembering snow as I remember sun.

LANDSCAPE OF VIOLENCE

Where racial memories, like snakes,
Coil above children as they play,
And every brown and white child wakes
Beside a sloughed-off love one day;

Where politics like hailstorms ride
And tear the future from the trees,
And every rider caught outside
Must pray between his horse's knees.

VOLUBILIS, NORTH AFRICA

South of the fabled pillars of Hercules
Where, among hills, the morning glory throngs,
Phoenician traders built Volubilis
Not with their hands but with their chaffering tongues.

The Carthaginian morning slid away
On stone-crushed oil from olive trees.
The stolid Romans spent their half a day
In pasting up prosaic memories

In huge stone albums: bath and victory arch,
Virgins, and dogs, and fish from the Great Sea
That once their fathers passed. How quiet the march
Of century on stealthy century –

Till Islam came, and tongues began again,
The tongues of faith that talked the tribesmen down,
That talked the townsmen out across the plain,
And argued city walls from uncut stone.

MARY MORISON WEBSTER

ILLI MORITURI

They do not care, the dying, whether it be dawn or dusk or
      daylight full and clear;
With eye ranging the familiar room unfamiliarly, they greatly
      dare,
Dismissing this and that with indifference, seeing through
      and beyond everything and those they hold dear,
Rejecting reality with a gesture that is not even complete,
      stripping stark and bare
All importance, acknowledging neither routine nor custom,
      not the milkboy's knock,
Nor the postman's round, nor the weather, reported in the
      papers cloudy or fair;
Detached, lifted for ever beyond the tyranny of Time, the
      imposition of the clock,
They hoist sails, the dying, they weigh anchor, they go out
      on a little breath, they do not care.

THE QUIET OF THE DEAD

The quiet of the dead
Is as the peace of stones;
They lie dust-comforted,
In their still house of bones.

Some gentle, deep content
Their timeless slumber yields;
Such quiet as is lent
To stones in winter fields.

I SET ASIDE

I set aside the things I wear,
Beads, silk, and mundane stuff;
Still my anxious body's there,
I can not get bare enough.

Not till I shed flesh and bone,
Divest myself of clay, I'll be
Quite sufficiently alone
For mine ownself's company.

GRASS

The grass hath such a simple faith,
And such strong power to heal,
It takes no certain heed of death,
But sets its single seal
On this year's grave, to weave it one,
Nor spares itself in bother,
Till it have made each green cocoon
Exactly like its brother.

THE SECRET

One keeps a secret for me,
That shall not now be told,
Though days stretch to Infinity
And all Time be unrolled.

Unless dead lip to lip
In ghostly syllable
Repeat it, or grass gossip,
None shall now tell it.

THE OX

This animal, this sleek and beautiful ox ambling along the
pleasant road,
Is being led to the slaughter; a noose is about his head;
Is being led to the slaughter, to an unspeakable place of
horror and blood,
In an hour or two, in a few hours at the most, he will be dead.

In the meantime, he walks lazily, contentedly sniffing the
dust,
Delicately patterned still and darkly, with the drops of the
baffled storm,
His hooves slipping heavily in his ease, his head, with its
mild eyes, out-thrust,
His flanks shaken with their own weight, spattered oozily
with dung still living and warm.

An ox, most patient of beasts and most innocent.
His warm, brown glance appraises this and that fearfully as
he proceeds;
Wherefore he travels this road he understands not, nor
whither he is being sent;
Turning from side to side, he displays a troubled interest in
the lush borders of grass and the flowering weeds.

Yet in an hour or two, in a few hours at the most, he will be
dead,
Will have suffered the final indignity at the hands of man in
a pen of blood,
His quivering flanks stilled for ever on a dreadful floor, his
nozzle red,
His cries, living and terrible still, hovering above the place
where he stood.

Surely, although it remains unrecorded, along the hot roads
   to Jerusalem,
Christ paused in the dust, viewing sorrowfully the herds and
   the terrified flocks,
Raised His voice often times, in anger and protest, beholding
   them,
Was moved to pity at sight of the sweating camel, wept for
   the lamb taken for slaughter, bemoaned the trapped
   fox.

And, watching the fishes tilting and tumbling in lively terror
   under His eyes,
Freeing themselves from the harsh nets, slipping and spilling
   in a heap of silver on the quiet sand,
Winced, unsuspected by Peter, above them, knowing how
   hardly even the smallest thing dies,
Troubled greatly in spirit by their glittering anguish, by the
   caperings of distress, by the spent leapings from
   the hand.

O Son of Man, surely indeed Thou grievest for such, and
   for all things of creation, of whatever kind,
Since even I do sorely grieve, and today stand on this roadside
   in the noonday light,
Lost and incredulous, staring down at a pattern of hooves in
   a great darkness of mind;
The ox, straining at his rope, bellowing loudly at last, breaking into a little run, passed from my sight.

EDWARD VINCENT SWART

TIRED OF EATING KISSES

Tired of eating kisses and the arms that gad,
I went walking with a more elaborate myth.
Went out of town with a cynical mouth,
The self satcheled on shoulder and an eye on good.

Was pleased as a Jill the first day on field.
Watching clouds smoulder, moving among trees,
The beetles ticking till the day had failed,
I chewing the grass as pleased as these.
And pleased on the fifth, a large day on field.
With what an abundant rhetoric
The white birds flourished and flowed to a rick!

But on the tenth day a want was foaled.
Under the neglected rib a bitter leaf.
Sight shut to a field where there wasn't any meaning.
An itch in the wind, and a white bird waiting one morning
Hunched on the gable, ready to leave.
Sharper and sharper the south side froze
Choking the grass. Desire muttered,
Protecting her throat over the last fuse.
In the deep pond no wish mattered.

The compass is broken, the mouth slack as a wound,
Which way, which way, with nothing on shoulder?
The grip gone on good and the eyes loose in the wind,
Which way, which way, with hope hard as a boulder?

CASEY JONES

Casey Jones has left today,
The decision was made in a desperate way,
Short as a wire and quick as a plane
And he isn't going to see any of you again.
There was no kind of good in staying on
When the delight was gone.

His hand at the welding was unsteady for months,
And the boss came very near sacking him once.
No rain for weeks: the old mower in pawn,
It was an impossible pastime cutting the lawn.
There was no kind of good in staying on
When the delight was gone.

Cries in the head were making him light,
He found it difficult sleeping at night,
The warmth of the women was a shocking reward,
And their unfortunate wishes were growing weird.
There was no kind of good in staying on
When the delight was gone.

O where did he head for? The wind in the wood,
And the goat on the tether was coughing up blood,
The clock on the church was pointing at ten
As he passed by the women and left the men.
There was no kind of good in staying on
When the delight was gone.

O where was he going? He didn't quite know,
For vague as a bandage the infected go,
And the mind must follow the deceived decision
Of the night before and the dream's incision.
There was no kind of good in staying on
When the delight was gone.

DOROTHEA SPEARS

BEGETTING

To be a birth there must be a begetting:
Immaculate, perhaps, but there must be
Begetting, a preparation and a setting
For concupiscent immortality.
Within the manifested form of mind
Or any substance, to achieve a birth
There must be an acceptance, a defined
Contactual point to vivify the earth.
A spark that fathers the innate desire.
Resemblances, revealing derivation,
Developing, disclose the latent sire.

It is the begetting sets the pattern firm
And gods are not begot from devils' sperm.

ADÈLE NAUDÉ

AFRICA

It speaks in voices varying with the wind;
To and fro the swirling accents veer.
The murmurs rise and breaking, fling
The spindrift of their phrases on the air.

We listen in but from this scattering
Of unfamiliar sounds upon the ear
We draw no meaning till the whorl of shell
Receiving, unifies and then we hear

Deep-throated warnings from an ocean bell,
Telling in tones that were not heard before
Of great seas moving darkly to a swell
And breakers thundering upon a shore.

PORTRAIT

Separately I still recall
The features as I knew them once;
The eyes, the way the lids would fall
To slant that gay and vivid glance;

And all between the brow and chin,
And how the head was held and framed,
The features closely woven in
By unifying line and plane.

I thought the memory proofed for time
In knowing warp and weft by heart;
Yet now the whole eludes my mind
As the old, old fabric falls apart.

FROM A VENETIAN SEQUENCE

The Ancient Song

Down the centuries, eternal
Primavera drifts along
Where glassblowers still flute out crystal
Lilies in their ancient song.

Anachronism

The gondola gives way to speed-boat
Yet Today they cannot catch,
Though Venice proudly wears a robot
As a child a birthday watch.

THE UNPOSSESSED

Still drifting together
    Out of the past
A cloud to its shadow
    Tethered fast.

I cast you from me,
    Image I've wrought,
But surely still binds
    The line of thought.

Now taut, now loose,
    Now vague and then clear,
When farthest away
    I find you near.

I fear no loss
    Though never at rest;
None has yet lost
    The unpossessed.

THE IDIOT

Still in an amorphous world she moves
As featureless as the landscape of her mind
Where sorrows, hates and loves have never grooved
Their scars nor moulded contours of design.

Softly she floats as though the indrawn breath
Of birth were held and still to be expired,
But when at last the tide sweeps her to death,
Then will she greet the new world with her cry?

ROBERT DEDERICK

ROBBEN ISLAND

Out there, with little else to do,
A man might spend a year or two
Holding within his splendid view

A mountain mutable, no less
Than the city of changefulness
Crooked in its cradling caress;

For there's a third-degree, a fray
Of time and tide fretting away
From Rocklands round to Grainger Bay;

But slowly, slow as time is to
A man with little else to do
But gaze and gaze on a splendid view.

KAROO TOWN

Reflected in the pensioner's eye
Beside us at the Post Office grille –
This corner sixty years gone by,
A bulge of sandbags, snarls of wire;
His father falls there, kicks, is still.
Taller today, the same trees sigh
Beside the gridded car-park where
His uncle gave the order to fire.

We think how today's long-headed men,
Turning from tears and terror, might
Set up their marvels here – how then
A city of squares and chiming hours
And fountains playing day and night
Might drum with rain again and again;
All round the waving horizon wheat
And forests and a flood of flowers.

But one is dead, the other must wait;
The present is our urgent care;
Our simple purpose one to create
That humming vacuum for the mind
Where a private world of prickly pear,
Donga, drift and cattlegate
Winds into our speedometer,
Runs out, and streams away behind.

F. TEMPLETON PRINCE

SOLDIERS BATHING

The sea at evening moves across the sand.
Under a reddening sky I watch the freedom of a band
Of soldiers who belong to me. Stripped bare
For bathing in the sea, they shout and run in the warm air;
Their flesh worn by the trade of war, revives
And my mind towards the meaning of it strives.

All's pathos now. The body that was gross,
Rank, ravenous, disgusting in the act or in repose,
All fever, filth and sweat, its bestial strength
And bestial decay, by pain and labour grows at length
Fragile and luminous. 'Poor bare forked animal',
Conscious of his desires and needs and flesh that rise and fall,
Stands in the soft air, tasting after toil
The sweetness of his nakedness: letting the sea-waves coil
Their frothy tongues about his feet, forgets
His hatred of the war, its terrible pressure that begets
A machinery of death and slavery,
Each being a slave and making slaves of others: finds that he
Remembers lovely freedom in a game
Mocking himself, and comically mimics fear and shame.

He plays with death and animality.
And reading in the shadows of his pallid flesh, I see
The idea of Michelangelo's cartoon
Of soldiers bathing, breaking off before they were half done
At some sortie of the enemy, an episode
Of the Pisan wars with Florence. I remember how he showed
Their muscular limbs that clamber from the water,
And heads that turn across the shoulder, eager for the
    slaughter,

74

Forgetful of their bodies that are bare,
And hot to buckle on and use the weapons lying there.
– And I think too of the theme another found
When, shadowing men's bodies on a sinister red ground,
Another Florentine, Pollaiolo,
Painted a naked battle: warriors, straddled, hacked the foe,
Dug their bare toes into the ground and slew
The brother-naked man who lay between their feet and drew
His lips back from his teeth in a grimace.

They were Italians who knew war's sorrow and disgrace
And showed the thing suspended, stripped: a theme
Born out of the experience of war's horrible extreme
Beneath a sky where even their air flows
With *lacrimae Christi*. For that rage, that bitterness, those
    blows,
That hatred of the slain, what could it be
But indirectly or directly a commentary
On the Crucifixion? And the picture burns
With indignation and pity and despair by turns,
Because it is the obverse of the scene
Where Christ hangs murdered, stripped, upon the Cross. I
    mean,
That is the explanation of its rage.

And we too have our bitterness and pity that engage
Blood, spirit, in this war. But night begins,
Night of the mind: who nowadays is conscious of our sins?
Though every human deed concerns our blood,
And even we must know, that nobody has understood,
That some great love is over all we do,
And that is what has driven us to this fury, for so few
Can suffer all the terror of that love:
The terror of that love has set us spinning in this groove
Greased with our blood.
               These dry themselves and dress,

Combing their hair, forget the fear and shame of nakedness.
Because to love is frightening we prefer
The freedom of our crimes. Yet, as I drink the dusky air,
I feel a strange delight that fills me full,
Strange gratitude, as if evil itself were beautiful,
And kiss the wound in thought, while in the west
I watch a streak of red that might have issued from Christ's
  breast.

THE QUESTION

And so we too came where the rest have come,
To where each dreamed, each drew, the other home
From all distractions to the other's breast,
Where each had found, each was, the wild bird's nest.
For that we came, and knew that we must know
The thing we knew of but we did not know.

We said then, What if this were now no more
Than a faint shade of what we dreamed before?
If love should here find little joy or none,
And done, it were as if it were not done,
Would we not love still? What if none can know
The thing we know of but we do not know?

For we know nothing but that, long ago,
We learnt to love God whom we cannot know.
I touch your eyelids that one day must close,
Your lips as perishable as a rose:
And say that all must fade, before we know
The thing we know of but we do not know.

THE OLD AGE OF MICHELANGELO

Sometimes the light falls here too as at Florence
Circled by low hard hills, or in the quarry
Under its half-hewn cliffs, where that collection
Of pale rough blocks, still lying at all angles on the dust-white
    floor
Waits, like a town of tombs.
                    I finish nothing I begin.
And the dream sleeps in the stone, to be unveiled
Or half-unveiled, the lurking nakedness;
Luminous as a grapeskin, the cold marble mass
Of melted skeins, chains, veils and veins,
Bosses and hollows, muscular convexities,
Supple heroic surfaces, tense drums
And living knots and cords of love:
– Sleeps in the stone, and is unveiled
Or half-unveiled, the body's self a veil,
By the adze and the chisel, and the mind
Impelled by torment.
                In the empty quarry
The light waits, and the tombs wait,
For the coming of a dream.

*

The power with which I imagine makes these things,
This prison:
And while the dream stirs in the stone, wakes in its chains,
Sometimes I think that I have spent my whole life making
    tombs,
And even those are unfinished. And yet, chafing,
Sadly closed there, in a rich bare case
Of bodily loveliness like solid sleep,
One sees the soul that turns
Waking, stretched on her side as if in pain, and how she sees
Browed like the dawn, the dark world

– Like a sulky pale cold louring dawn –
Loathing her hope of fruit, the pure bare flank:
Or else one sees her sunk in rest,
Letting her worn head droop over her empty body
And the much-pulled breasts hang dry,
Fallen, with long flat nipples.

And there is always
Some victor and some vanquished, always the fierce sub-
    stance
And the divine idea, a drunkenness
Of high desire and thought, or a stern sadness:
And while it rests or broods or droops,
There will be always some great arm or shoulder
To incur or to impose some heavy torment,
There will be always the great self on guard, the giant
Reclined and ominous,
With back half-turned, hunched shoulder
And the enormous thigh
Drawn up as if disdainful,
Almost the bare buttock offered:
There will be always
A tall Victory with beaten Age
Doubled beneath its bent knee, but ignoring
(The naked proud youth bending aside
His vacuous burning brow and wide
Beautiful eyes and blank lips) but ignoring
The sad sordid slave, the old man.

*

And now I have grown old,
It is my own life, my long life I see
As a combat against nature, nature that is our enemy
Holding the soul a prisoner by the heel;
And my whole anxious life I see
As a combat with myself, that I do violence to myself,
To bruise and beat and batter
And bring under

My own being,
Which is an infinite savage sea of love.

*

For you must know I am of all men ever born
Most inclined to love persons, and whenever I see someone
Who has gifts of mind and body, and can say or show me
    something
Better than the rest,
Straightway I am compelled
To fall in love with him, and then I give myself
Up to him so completely, I belong no longer to myself,
He wresting from me
So great part of my being, I am utterly
Bewildered and distraught, and for many days know nothing
Of what I am doing or where I am.
– Young green wood spits in burning,
Dry wood catches the flame: and I become now
An old man with a face like wrinkled leather, living alone,
And with no friends but servants,
Parasites, bad disciples puffed up by my favours, or else
    Popes,
Kings, cardinals or other patrons, being as for myself alone
Either a lord or subject, either with my gossips and buffoons
And clumsy fawning relatives; or towards you and such as
    you,
Whom I adore, an abject:
                    Messer THOMAS

CAVALIERE
I am naked in that sea of love
Which is an infinite savage glowing sea,
Where I must sink or swim. Cold, burning with sorrow,
I am naked in that sea and know
The sad foam of the restless flood
Which floats the soul or kills, and I have swum there
These fifty years and more,
And never have I burned and frozen

More than I have for you,
Messer Tommaso.

*

Moon-cold or sun-hot, through what alternations
Of energy, long languor,
Periods of mad defiance, periods of fear, flight, misery
Cowering darkly,
Moon-cold or sun-hot, love that grips
Sun, moon, eternal hatred
Eternal hope and pain, packed close in one man's body,
And drawn, leaning to others.
                                And one other:
Grey eyes float in the dry light
That might draw Venus' car, moving at morning
Grey eyes through dry dark shadows, floating
Over the blocked ways, the despair,
And opening wide lids, irises
More starlike than the stars, purer than they, alive in the
        pale air,
Fire, life in thin dry air
Drawing the soul out at the mouth
Beauty in triumph,
My defeat.

*

– I am always alone, I speak to no one
But that shabby Bernardo, nor do I wish to:
Trudging up and down Italy, wearing out my shoes and life,
Toiling still to grow poorer, ugly, sad,
Proud, narrow, full of unfulfilled desires!

Yet I have come to Rome, rich in its ruins, and for the last
        time,
As if I made to cross a little stream dry-foot
That had divided us, and yet again, for the last time
My dream grows drunk within me,
And opens its great wings and like an eagle

Wild naked perfect pure soars from its nest.
Almost I am persuaded, almost, that it is possible,
My love, like anybody's love, is possible.
My eye stares on your face, and my old mind
Soars naked from its cliff, and thinks to find
– Drunk with illumination as the sky itself is drunken
Or a dry river-bed with light –
The wild path to its thought, for all is passion
Here, even cogitation, and it climbs and clambers, floats and
    flings
And hovers, it is thrust up, it is hurled
Throbbing into the stillness,
Rapt, carried by the blissful air
Borne up, rebuffs and buffets
– Having hurled
The dead world far below it –
Stretches out long rapturous claws and wings,
Stiff as with agony, shakes as with tenderness
And dives and hovers at you, swoops and aches
To stun, caress
And beat you to your knees,
Clutches and clings,

– As if it would grow one with you and carry
Up the solitary sky
That strange new beautiful identity,
Where it might never fade or melt or die!
And many things
Are put about and taken up and spread abroad
About Michelangelo, poor old man, but when I
Come to you, I care nothing
For honour or the world, I only care
To look long on your face, and let
The dream soar from its nest. For do I know
Myself, what I should mean? I only know
That if I had those wings, not in a dream,
And I could open, beat those wings;

If I could clutch you in the claws of dream,
And take you up with me in loneliness
To the roof-tree, angle of heaven, vault
Of exquisite pale buffeted glare:
I should gain or regain
The heaven of that high passion, pallor, innocence
– I should gain or regain
The sole pure love, and fence it with my wings.

*

But my two eyes
Are empty, having wept, and my skin stretched
Like an old hide over my dry bones, and my face
Grown flat and timorous, broken,
Loving or having loved this dream.
And the light fades from the sky, the dream dies in the stone
Slowly, I finish nothing I begin, and in my evening
Last torments and last light, torn hesitations
Between desire and fear, between desire and my disdain
– Emerging into dusky rooms, high walls, rich architecture
And the tawny roofs of Rome. For this love discovers only
The world's desert and death, the dusty prison
Where we have shut ourselves, or the sky shuts us.

Fades the light, and below there
I lie, an old man like a fallen god propped up:
My eyes close, and my head hangs,
Heavy as if with love-drink or with dreams,
And from my old thick swagging side
Pours forth a marble river. Overhead floats
A face, two brilliant eyes
That make the whole world pale,
Floating, and that great nobleness,
That great despising, of the mind
To which the beautiful is as the felt heat
Of the fire of the eternal.

Do not forget the poor old man.

JACK COPE

———

ROCK PAINTING

A leather-skinned wrinkled old man
old hunter yellow as the stones
from the rock he hears the rain talk
    hyena cracking bones

A song with five words has a sway
the lion sees its head in the river
a song is a flame in the thorn-fire
    the story is forever

Five words shuffle in the dance ring
five dancers whose feet never tire
they sing of the great grey cat
    his tail caught on fire

What is the shadow dance saying
to the hunter? he will not forget
a rain-woman talked in the firelight
    the small moon set

The eland is standing just so
thorns in the fireplace piled
the word is an arrow without death
    song a sleeping child

Listen to the cough at the waterhole
mantis marks a shadow on the stone
the story is a hunter returning
    who does not come alone

His trail is through the stars forever
white ash thrown in the sky
they know, the fire and the dancers
    do they know he will die?

THE FLYING FISH

For Ingrid

The level ocean lies immeasurably blind
swept through green deeps to glutinous weed.

But the flying fish, how they leap away
in water-flashes to the enamelled sun!
They break along the foam-lipped chorus
of sea-swells. Mysterious
the sounds they loosen, arrows
singing on the air and lost:
Mysterious the glass-winged birds
of the long blind sea.

On the storm-swung streams they ride
over free oceans over the locked ice
the groans of midnight fires
and moons returning on the tide.
Light as great winged travellers
of the endless South
urgent as birth
from gloomed fishweed and the dead underwave
the flying fish sing to light.

IF YOU COME BACK

If you come back ever
if you come in the smoky Decembers
sweeping out of estranged eyes
all the strange and magnetic stars one by one
and drop them, faint and flawed diamonds
picked from the waxed velvet of the sorting-sky
if you come again wearing the sun
like a burning-glass, what shall I say?

If you are a child again
with a long thin body and ice skin
body of the small white tulips
body of magnesium and hidden fire
if you come in the sea sound
the sirens and the minute-gun on the hill
if you stop counting – what shall I say?

If the fallen rocks fuse
and no oceans lie prone to the sliding keels
Atlantic empty as a sigh
and the cathedrals stand hollow of dreams
and prayer, and you come wondering
at the mystery of virgins and canals
and the antelope raising wet eyes
into the mouth of the night
if your heart beats again –

Sense of the arum lily
sense of the crimson and blueness
camelia of words, the hours clashing
together like ice on the autumn river,
flowers without roots, flowers of air:
if you should come seeking by its scent
in the grass the secret babiaantjie
what should I say?

The ribbed sand dunes
shrill plaintive under my tread;
if I dance like the tall shy rain-cloud
have I not captured the rain?
Desert of the stone rose, desert of ash-flowers.
If you should count time ever again
by the clock of the Cross, scent on petals
blood again in the corn, if you walk
gold and fierce blue over the endless Spring
it is because of the words
because I have gone silent and distant
    bearing the seed of my words.

SONS

They say: He lives with colours
and moulds daring forms, his mind
runs on dreams and banners, fearless
voyages, his inward gaze brave and kind.

And he, ah he can figure keenly;
strange words, subtle images stay
easily in his brazen calculating head,
eyes astonishing or sad and grey.

One makes new conquests, wild with courage;
his eager ship strains too slow to sail
and in his full heart pure and repurified
he knows that failing he can never fail.

And this tow-headed true inheritor
of all venturers moves his squared stones
and batters down bars, lifts the white sand
and in one grain sees the world's bones.

Take nothing from them, the small things,
the smell of summer on the melon sea,
a half-round pebble, time, unchanging blue
and winter frosts: Let the small day be.

SAPPHO

Always she goes like a captured wild bird
and lifts her red mouth, but remembering
the first exquisite flight, holds back her words.

Sick of evenings, sick of the black ships
she loosens the warp off the harnessed loom
and wanders back, a child, to a dark tide:
surf-sounds caught in a shell,
in the veins the blue water's slide.

Slow break and break along her blood,
the gulls breast out in a grey flight,
a star shrinks on her eye and the shore
unrolls a nautilus of crumbling light.

The rock path is long and she climbs alone.
The girls call to her from a walled yard
and she turns to share a burst pomegranate.
But the lips in the water she kissed – were hers,
her mouth blooms with a beloved name, her own.

TANIA VAN ZYL

TWO WOMEN

In the corner the fire made a place.
It chuckled and purred alive and content
with this fragment and that; it ate of this
and ate of that. Two women lived beside
the fire and tended but mended not the draught.
They spoke of the world, the colour and
sounds that sifted and twisted through street
and house. The walls were alive with
peacock eyes. Across the faded Persian mat
there rode a general while by the fire
a traveller sat. One woman painted
golden leaves and golden buds; one told of
temples in walnut groves; of lovers who
sought the Taurus snows; of dreaming wings
on the Rann of Kutch; forgotten gods that
hidden sleep, deep and alone in russet shade.
One never knew in the arm of fire if
one played that night in druid glade
or the stone heart probed of a Syrian tower.

THE MAN WITH THE HOLLOW BREAST

That knot in the wood if wood
should knot
to indicate the rift obstinate
breaking the clean-fleshed surface.
In one piece cut of oak, yet rifted oak;
the man sturdy stood
with burrowing mole-toes.

With square thumbs like engrafted
parts for other uses –
the shapely mouth shaped to tell
but telling what in telling
is not forgotten and not been, some
tender milk-weed tale.

Or he stood on arctic edge –
ice-numbed,
and blocked his head with frozen
whale-building dream,
a Jonah riding with a lashing rod
in blessed fantasy coming to dredge
for plankton in rich phantom seas.

His algaed eyes saw what eyes might
see if they
had power to bring the loaded ship
on monsoon wing and there unload
the riches that would make of him
the richest one that ever such a load
could find but that was not to be.

THE ROPE

What scope
is there where
ends the rope?
For between this swing
and nothing
life is measured.
So little
then it matters
what is treasured.

THE HOUSE

The house with coarse stuccoed
brow stands abrupt
at verging bank, thrusting
knees to the river.
Stone pines fan the sun
from her face.

Tortuous and narrow roads
lead beyond to pour
as from a bottle the walker
into the grave.
At the roadhouse many play
at cards with war and death.

Couples in the dance hall
spin, fling, break and
twine; at dawn vomited
into the green street.
Some like sweat-loaded gnats
buzz out in the sun
an enervated passion.

The house is empty – white-collared
crows in greater and greater
numbers gather and cursing
are cemented by common design
to invade the house.

THE HORSES OF MARINI

The horses of Marini ride
side by side
some fast some slow.
Others stand and fully take
the landscape in their eye.

A few over shoulder stare
at man who solid sits
or flinches back.
More wild and thin the horses
grow carved by the wind.
Almost headless
with whittled ears
their flanks as bat-wings
grip the sky.

The horses of Marini go
we do not know where.
Sometimes the rider
is the horse, now forward
and then back leans,
or like a pewter bird
launches with planet shape
on some far spacial course
alone. Horse and man
affrighted are, a parting
tips them to the void's rim.

Horses over broken
landscapes riding
your eyes are of starlight
your flanks are of fire.
The rider you carry is dead.
Who laments in the sky
with a song of birds?
It is the riders willing
each other to die.
Blue and red horses,
over the cruel blades
of the mountain, beyond
the fierce-armed furnace,
flee and know in
the blindness of the rider
his bondage to death.

Riderless horses
with comet-flared nostrils
where do you go?
With rolling and turning
your body is round.
Driven and pursued,
staked and loosed,
when will the unfathomed cave
of a thousand shades stable you?

SHE WAITED

She waited as one
deciding time had created
a human pause to fill
with ringing sound,
with colour fanning
from some spectral palette,
or cloud sculpted form.
She waited.

Who saw her sitting
on a stone crowned peak,
face held in palms?
Her mind lost to the near
and to the distant
an ear travelling to infinity.

Where is she? they ask.
No foot print discover,
only her shape solid
squared in ice waited.
The pause she was,
that interval held.
At what time would the sun
melting tilt her into the stream?

ANTHONY DELIUS

DEAF-AND-DUMB SCHOOL

On the black tarmac playground dark
Nuns, a white statue of the Virgin watch
Bare feet of the muted children jerk
And scuffle over endless silence. Such

Is their element. Though I have heard
Them flute like evening swallows in the sky
The sounds were sad, irrelevant, absurd
And could not pierce the silences of play,

Nor break the glass that frames their world.
A soundless quality of painting grips
A small boy leaning from a bench enthralled
In thoughts that dance on other finger-tips.

One with the cry and stiffness of a crane
Dances before a dumb-struck clientele,
Beyond, some cheerless footballers bemoan
A speechless player's bungled goal.

And all around communication glimmers
From hand to eye, and each attentive face
Turns to a dream of mimicry and murmurs,
Like songless planets signalling through space.

Sound there is, but silence underlies
The fire-flies of gesture. One cannot catch
Exactly what the muffled outcry says,
Or what it is the nuns and children watch.

Silence like a window shows the room
Of minds that make their signs and mouth their cries,
But what leans out to touch you from the dream
Only the white statue and the darkness realize.

LADY ANNE BATHING

I have grown used to the retreat of seasons,
South-Easter, slow hail of different stars,
I can confront the threat of noosed horizons
Accept Napoleon's or another's wars

Are all my own, and no war has an end
Though evil changes sides. See, waters whiten
On the mountain face, whisper rage, descend
Till they step, pretty as a leopard's kitten

To fill my pool. In Town I dance my reel,
The Lady or the Poet, whatever is expected.
Existence caged in rooms or on parole
Will play the proper part that's to be acted.

The Burghers watch me from their placid lust
That has no naked eye. The officers
Dispense official gaiety, hate thrust
Away beneath the weeping chandeliers.

But dread of tame civility will grow,
Silk hiss against the flesh – until I flee
The twinkling clavichord and wine to show
My nakedness in hostage to a tree.

I stand here pale upon the mountain, dream
In panic at the bare baptismal step,
See water take my body without shame
And merge the shadow as the substance in its lap,

Wait poised above the sky within the shock,
The ecstasy caught in this cornered river,
And in exploding quiet watch the rock,
The tree, the peak and all beyond it shiver.

FOOTNOTE

Cetewayo, Chief of the Zulus,
Enduring injustice in Cape Town,
Wrote to little Saul Solomon,
Who wept for a drowned daughter,
'One of your branches has withered . . .'

How good to know it now,
Long after grief and gesture,
That an impounded Black monarch
Sent a White politician
A green sprig of simile.

THE GAMBLERS

The Coloured long-shore fishermen unfurl
their nets beside the chilly and unrested sea,
and in their heads the little dawn-winds whirl
some scraps of gambling, drink and lechery.

Barefoot on withered kelp and broken shell,
they toss big baskets on the brittle turf,
then with a gambler's bitter patience still
slap down their wagering boat upon the surf.

Day flips a golden coin – but they mock it.
With calloused, careless hands they reach
deep down into the sea's capacious pocket
and pile their silver counters on the beach.

INTUITION

In a climate where
Nothing grows
But a slow and tame despair
In all one knows

Now and then a day arrives
Out of no time
One can recognize, lives,
Offers the old dream

To be proud again, little else
Can we cherish
To make the praying pulse
A growing parish.

But that day also ends
As all others do,
The sun goes down, the wind's
Self says No.

SHADOW

Shadow, killer of doves
and mossies, has fallen,
and what counter of deaths
has measured his end?

That a black cat with golden
eyes died on a green lawn,
a small boy wept for him,
a woman mourned his white

claws, what in the traffic
of stars, nations, signifies it
between some unimportant houses
a cat failed to make its way home?

Many cats will die, many
stars, countries fall, eyes
of just that gold widen
again in an alert face of night.

Perhaps the plump doves
will be one stalker the safer.
Such a minute gain in security
is hardly worth a feather

on the grass. Yet sunlight will be
more vacant for the loss
of that detachment from darkness
that blazed with its own suns.

Cleaning blood from his claws
in a treefork, coolly asleep
under hedges, he was his own
delight and solar system.

DISTANCE

The Gods of Africa regard me
From the edge of my suburban lawn.
They have the tall thick legs of tree-trunks,
And tiny white faces of the stars.

I do not grovel at their sprouting toes,
But stand in my Euclidian door
And hope the centuries of grass
Are far too wide to leap across.

THE THINKER

Round and round our lavatory
walks a depressed cricket
like a lonely manager
of a cement factory,

the huge cistern and bowl
and mysterious pipes above him,
and he worries, ticking with calculation,
troubled about production
and reproduction.

Every now and then, at unpredictable intervals,
comes darkness,
and seven-league boots, and enormous draperies
drop down from heaven,
and afterwards
a great roaring, an apocalypse of waters.

And the serpent holding the world
together unclenches its tail
and hisses – and boots and draperies
retreat reluctantly, thundering.

And the cricket thinks:
Well, there must be a rational explanation,
I suppose – but, all the same,
it seems bloody queer.

BRIEF FAREWELL

This was a love in which there was always
farewell. Farewell, my child, but always
and forever welcome, in which there will be
no departure, and always departure,
the train leaving, and the certainty

of return flung back by that heart-burrowing
whistle touching the skies and the nerves
with a shudder and leaving the distances
calling, and the empty station, the memory
of two red suitcases stacked on a seat.

Oh there was nothing final about them
but they prophesied finality in after-
images, spoke deep in me of the ultimate
farewell, and a turning away that would not
be forever, but would speak for forever

to know this time of completeness gone.

GUY BUTLER

COMMON DAWN

Submitting to a sentry's fate
I concentrate
    On the day's way of dawning –

Grey clouds brighten, birds awake,
Wings and singing shake
    The curtained silence of the morning.

As gentle as a bird, the breeze
Brushes the grass about my knees
    So softly that the dew remains

On every blade from here to where
Alien sentries, watching, share
    The view of fatal plains.

Alone, awake, I sense how still
Is the presence of a timeless hill
    How universal all this air,

Till I can hardly bear to face
Such sweet and subtle commonplace,
    The sunlight everywhere.

CAPE COLOURED BATMAN

As the slanting sun drowsed lazily
On the terraced groves of Tuscany
At last I found him, back to a trunk:
Nelson, my batman, the bastard, drunk.

On the grass beneath an olive tree
His legs lay splayed in a khaki V
And all his body, relaxed, at ease,
Head thrown back, while over his knees
Strumming the banjo his yellow hands
Stirred all his sorrow from four steel strands.

His melancholy cries from Hollywood,
'Where the coyotes cry' or 'Lady be Good',
In that declining light awoke
A tenderness for the stupid bloke,
So happy his sorrow, so at ease
Strumming the strings across his knees.

No doubt a pirate Javanese
From Malacca Straits or Sunda Seas
Shaped those almond eyes of his;

A Negress from the Cameroons –
Bought for brandy, sold for doubloons –
Gave him a voice that wails and croons;

An eagle Arab trading far
From Hadramaut to Zanzibar
Left him a nose like a scimitar;

A Bush-girl from the Namaqua sands
Bequeathed him bird-like, restless hands
Stirring his sorrow from four steel strands;

While English, Dutch and Portuguese
Sick of biscuits and sodden cheese
Put in at the Tavern of the Seas,

Northerners warm in the Southern night
Drank red Cape brandy, and got tight –
And left him a skin that's almost white.

This is the man the Empires made
From lesser breeds, the child of Trade
Left without hope in History's shade;

Shouldered aside into any old place,
Damned from birth by the great disgrace,
A touch of the tar-brush in his face.

Under pines, mimosas and mango trees
Strewn through the world lie men like these:
Drunk crooning voices, banjos on knees.

He fell asleep in a vinous mist,
Star in his mouth, bottle in fist,
The desperate, maudlin hedonist.

But the pathos of the human race
Sainted his drunken, relaxed face;
And a warm dusk wind through the olive trees
Touched mute strings across his knees
With sorrows from the Seven Seas.

GIOTTO'S CAMPANILE

Alone in the atoning belfry how I grieve
For all the motley, heroic and appalling
Soldiers who squander scraps of rationed leave

Within you, City: grieve, recalling
How Dante at what bitter distance bled.
Then, upon the spiral stair, steel heels falling,

The well-shod feet of the soon-to-be dead:
 How casually they pause; note landmarks;
    curse the climb.
Hammers descend on the bronze above my head

To rivet us all to a pointless point in Time,
And over the town, trebles, twos and ones,
Shark-like shoals slip through the tidal chime,

Planes in flight, forming to swell the guns'
Staccato knell, tolling through acres of skies
For quivering loins and unengendered sons.

All sounds diminish, die. The far throb dies.
A grey sky waits for stars. No death is poured
Upon dim Florence, dusk-soft, drowsing in my eyes,

But bitterly, distantly, I bleed for the still adored
Now under terror and night – O vision city,
In all your campaniles which praised, implored,

None, none peals now, deep bells of love and pity.

MYTHS

Alone one noon on a sheet of igneous rock
I smashed a five-foot cobra's head to pulp;
Then, lifting its cool still-squirming gold
In my sweating ten separate fingers, suddenly
Tall aloes were also standing there,
Lichens were mat-red patches on glinting boulders,
Clouds erupted white on the mountains' edge,
All, all insisting on being seen.
Familiar, and terribly strange, I felt the sun
Gauntlet my arms and cloak my growing shoulders.

Never quite the same again
Poplar, oak or pine, no, none
Of the multifarious shapes and scents that breed
About the homestead, below the dam, along the canal,

Or any place where a European,
Making the most of a fistful of water, splits
The brown and grey with wedges of daring green –
Known as invaders now, alien,
Like the sounds on my tongue, the pink on my skin;
And, like my heroes, Jason, David, Robin Hood,
Leaving tentative footprints on the sand between
The aloe and the rock, uncertain if this
Were part of their proper destiny. Reading
Keats' *Lamia* and *Saint Agnes' Eve*

Beneath a giant pear tree buzzing with bloom
I glanced at the galvanized windmill turning
Its iron sunflower under the white-hot sky
And wondered if a Grecian or Medieval dream
Could ever strike root away from our wedges of green,
Could ever belong down there
Where the level sheen on new lucerne stops short:
Where aloes and thorns thrust roughly out
Of the slate-blue shales and purple dolerite.
Yet sometimes the ghosts that books had put in my brain
Would slip from their hiding behind my eyes
To take on flesh, the sometimes curious flesh
Of an African incarnation.

One winter dusk when the livid snow
On Swaershoek Pass went dull, and the grey
Ashbushes grew dim in smudges of smoke,
I stopped at the outspan place to watch,
Intenser as the purple shades drew down,
A little fire leaping near a wagon,
Sending its acrid smoke into the homeless night.
Patient as despair, eyes closed, ugly,
The woman stretched small hands towards the flames;
But the man, back to an indigo boulder,
Face thrown up to the sky, was striking
Rivers of sorrow into the arid darkness
From the throat of a battered, cheap guitar.

It seemed that in an empty hell
Of darkness, cold and hunger, I had stumbled on
Eurydice, ragged, deaf forever,
Orpheus playing to beasts that would or could not hear,
Both eternally lost to news or rumours of spring.

SURVEYOR

Cutting that jungle road from Lugardville
Everything went wrong. The road gangs
Always at the throats of the villagers
Who always overcharged them
For booze, and yams, and girls.
Many on both sides died bewitched.
Each pay day bred a bout of gambling
Followed by stabbings, frequently fatal.
Not to mention the normal snags, like malaria
And the run of tropical bugs. The Doctor himself went down,
All his quinine dumped in a swamp by a careless coon.

Superiors, equals, inferiors all advised:
Wait for new supplies, another dry season.
Pay the swobs off, man, don't be stubborn.
There's no disgrace. Listen to reason.

But I decided to try
Democracy, diplomacy.

So I called a full indaba of headman and of foremen
And sat like Solomon in my canvas chair between them,
In a clean bush-jacket and best topee,
With a drunken interpreter swaying behind my throne.
On my left
Nestling on mats in garments of skins,
Bush pagans, dignified, suspicious,
And one old Christian convert

In starched khaki shorts and lime-white shoes.
On my right
The invaders, the roadmakers, the breakers of custom:
A tall mine-boy with flashing aluminium helmet,
A chap in dungarees with ear plugs the size of saucers,
And a suave young slickie, lounge-suited for the occasion
Who thought he spoke Oxford English.

And they talked, they wrangled for hours
In a green nightmare beneath the windless trees.
At no point could any formula of mine
Find purchase to lever them into sense.
They heard failure in my voice.
I'd lost my grip and they saw it
In my fidgeting nicotined fingers.

Defeated, I rose from my canvas throne
Lifting a hand for silence.
I intended, at last, to dismiss them,
But instead, to my own surprise,
Ignoring the interpreter, I said
Crisply, in coolest English:
In any right-angled triangle
The square on the hypotenuse
Equals the sum of the squares on the other two sides.
In the following baffled silence
The forest ceased to frighten,
The swamps shrank back, afraid;
The demoralizing babel
Of voices and drowsy drums
Dimmed to a boring vibration.

I allowed myself one brief smile,
Inside I was rocking with laughter:
I laughed the Congo Basin to scorn,
I leered sideways at the Mountains of the Moon
I regarded the six thousand miles

Of the Great Rift Valley with amusement,
And I took up the whole Sahara
As a very small thing.
All Africa's black witch-doctors
All her white orators
All the dizzy word spinners of the world
Could not refute that proposition.

I laughed, got things in proportion,
I ceased to be intimidated.
They saw it, and accepted.
The road went through on time.

The Commies are using it now.

CHARLES EGLINGTON

THE VANQUISHED

With treble vivas and limp hedgerow flags
The children welcome us: again we meet
The fearful sons and daughters of defeat.
And through the town our dull compassion drags
The scarecrow of our greeting.
                                        Brown-eyed brat,
Your dusty face and sapless, sapling limbs
Start in my blood a wave of anger that
Breaks hotly on my eyes in spray that dims
Your hungry, haunted smile but cannot drown
The image of a child you bring to mind
Who might be mine: If ever, thin and brown,
She, too, must some day wait to find
Bread and forgiveness on the conquerors' way,
May they advance defeated – as today.

ARRIVAL AND DEPARTURE

The placid, rotted harbour has no voice
To bid departing travellers goodbye;
They, watching as land, sea and sky
Merge, are regretful of all things – the choice
That charts their steady course from day to day,
The port that lies behind, the one ahead,
The astrolabe of unrest that has led
Them north or south, but always the same way.

For strange each time the harbour reached, and far
The harbour that is home; each embarkation
Means farewell and every pilot-star
That winks the vessel to its destination
Burns briefly and the heart, anchored again,
Rocks on the tide, tugs at the anchor chain.

THE LOWVELD

The brown arms of the mothering plateau
Seem to restrain me here against a fall
Into the lambent sea of bush, below
This high blue cleft in the escarpment wall,
From which slow-rolling waves of febrile heat
Swirl up, to daze the mind with vertigo
And race the pulse with metronomic beat.

How many men have foundered in that sea
Between the Lebombos and where I now stand?
Lean, rufous trekkers, seeking legendary
Iconographs of lustre in the sand:
Who, when marooned at last in tents of shade
From ample fig or frugal fever tree,
Refused to curse the impulse they'd obeyed?

Like the old, mystic mariner who charted
His voyage in Isaiah, in their Bible
They found maps of Canaan and departed;
Trod down the frontier, gladly quit the tribal
Shelter of snug farm, aspiring town
And costive myth, to wander single-hearted
Towards the haze that covered the unknown.

Malaria, red suns and hunger burned
Their blood and substance; failing hope annealed
Their faith in miracles; privation turned
Them animal, and bird and beast revealed
The secret of the wilderness that guides
All rebel creatures, singular or spurned,
Along safe trails to water-holes and hides.

Fatigue became a solace, doubt a thirst
They slaked in lust for distances; some day
A charge of dawn would split the rim and burst
Upon the paradise of plains that they
Had seen beyond mirages of the haze
And over which, alone, they'd be the first
To lay the spoor of their diverging ways.

But, ever-shifting, the horizon swung
Its oceanic line ahead; until,
Each trekker knew contentment and unslung
His rucksack of illusion: steadfast still,
He could believe the prophecies of birds
And understand the cruel and lucid tongue
Directing the migration of the herds.

BUFFALO

In kraals of slanting shade the herd
Moves restively: flared nostrils vent
The cordite fumes of summer, snuff
The dung of slow diminishment.
Old sagas of migration vex
Their torpor with blood memories
Of boundless grazing, pools and hides,
Fights and strong seasonal increase.

Curved boss thrust down, imperial
In hump of shoulder, loop of horn,
A great bull hoofs the dust; his squat
Flanks twitch and rope with muscles worn
By treks and mating: master still
Of cows he sired and won, and hot
Young bulls, his signal temper draws
The phalanx round him in a knot.

Slow, tentative, the sickled heads
Are lifted; incandescent eyes
Reflect, beyond their range of sight,
The swelling thunder buds that rise
In soundless tumult to discharge
The storm; no fear or challenge cracks
Its whip-lash: dull, incurious,
They drop their heads and hunch their backs.

And by their sloth the old bull knows
His impotence: the lowing sky
Commands more sweetly, the breathing rain,
Than he can warn. In mute reply,
He stands defiantly to meet
The sleek new leader of the herd –
The Bull of Heaven charging down
To graze the pastures, tame and lourd.

LOURENÇO MARQUES

O mar salgado, quanto do teu sal
São lagrimas de Portugal!
Fernando Pessoa

Once, grave Laodicean profiteer,
This harbour welcomed neutral ships
And warring secrets: enemies,
Remote from where fierce, fatal loyalties
Strode armed with death, strolled casually
And mingled with shut faces and tight hearts
In this pacific city, open then
To an ocean menaced by their conflict.
In still blue waters of flamboyant shade
Intrigue and treason, treachery and hate
Fermented like paludal slime. In febrile dreams
The city shared the strangers' destiny.

Yet, in that tense neutrality
There was a brooding innocence:
The war was far away and though the sea
Might wash a blaze of fire from the night,
The city knew the probabilities.
Its lassitude was old and wise;
The ocean it confronted was
(As backward-looking, sad Pessoa knew)
Salt with the tears of Portugal;
The mother-country's wars had all been fought –
How could there ever come a time
For guilt, expatiation and remorse?

Now (many years have passed) I sit
In still blue waters of flamboyant shade
And muse as sad Pessoa never could:
I lack blood-knowledge of those bitter tears,
Those centuries when caravels

Caught storms of hazard in their sails
And left, in spastic writing on all maps,
Directions to the unknown worlds of earth;
The city, grown and prosperous,
Exalts in me no backward-looking thoughts –
It has the future's brooding innocence;
I sense another taut neutrality.
Its world, though growing old, is young,
Its rooted heritage is germinal;
Behind its tall, proud back a continent
Throws out a challenge, like the oceans once.

RUTH MILLER

PLANKTON

Remember the day the sea turned red:
The breakers ruddy as though the sun
Had fallen, Icarus-spent, too soon;
We watched it from a white dune

And marvelled that the changing element
Could be so changed. Russet-tinged,
The rollers crimsoned; but inshore
Were cats-eye green as before.

From floating seethe of miniscules,
A billion in each drop, the pale
Profusion blossomed rose again
In one far blood-red stain.

Breasting the inshore waves, we speared
Through them, cleansed and clean as air.
Huge seas lifted, took us, leaping,
By the hands, and drew us in;

Drew us further, deeper, into
And beyond the next and next
Massive, smooth, unclenching green.
One step more – we would have been

Engulfed beneath the swinging crests
Curving in a rush of rose.
Back we forced – the ominous tide
Away from us, flowered, and died.

Away from us, died too
The bright day, a fallen feather.
Apart, we left the strange sea
Within each other.

BIRDS

The lion, even when full of mud, with burrs
On his belly tangled, his great pads heavy
And cracked, sends such a message on the dry air
As makes all smaller animals wary, their fur
Rising in silken shivers, their horned heads
Up with the wind, reading its tragic story.

There is nothing majestic about death. Yet the king
Remains royal and knows it, is accepted
Though fled. Only the tiniest things –
The birds, whirr down from the tall sky, fling
Their feathered softnesses at shadows, dare to move
In his company, dare to sing.

Suppose a million birds could once shake loose
From the tops of trees from the white horizon,
Veering in a soft outflinging noose,
Clouds in their clouds, lightning in their claws,
To peck out his sagging heart. How royally they
        would bedizen
His beggarman bones with the charity of their wings.

PENGUIN ON THE BEACH

Stranger in his own element,
Sea-casualty, the castaway manikin
Waddles in his tailored coat-tails. Oil

Has spread a deep commercial stain
Over his downy shirtfront. Sleazy, grey,
It clogs the sleekness. Far too well

He must recall the past, to be so cautious:
Watch him step into the waves. He shudders
Under the froth, slides, slips, on the wet sand,

Escaping to dryness, dearth, in a white cascade,
An involuntary shouldering off of gleam.
Hands push him back into the sea. He stands

In pained and silent expostulation.
Once he knew a sunlit, leaping smoothness,
But close within his head's small knoll, and dark

He retains the image: oil on sea,
Green slicks, black lassos of sludge
Sleaving the breakers in a stain-spread scarf.

He shudders now from the clean flinching wave,
Turns and plods back up the yellow sand,
Ineffably weary, triumphantly sad.

He is immensely wise: he trusts nobody. His senses
Are clogged with experience. He eats
Fish from his Saviour's hands, and it tastes black.

LONG SINCE LAST

Long since last I tried remembering
You, such singing solstice-swings away.
Now it's another winter and the best
Of me has shadowed with the sun.
The cold sunlight slants into the room
So late, staying so short a while, that I
Light the fire early, watch the grate

Bar into gold and creep up near the glow
To warm abandoned hands that once could lie
On a cold night in the heat of your gaze
As though there was no bitter wind, as though
Spring would be always coming and I would utter
Always the words that now sleep in a frost-
Bound sleep, deep in unblessed silences, and lost
O lost to the bliss of any more remembering.

STERKFONTEIN

The Sterkfontein caves, Transvaal, were the scene of Dr
Broom's famous discovery of the skeletal remains of
prehistoric man.

Our caves do not go Boom! and make one nervy,
For they are underground, and dark and hard,
And high up near a Scot a Van der Merwe
Has notched his name, and left the crystal scarred.

Our caves say nothing in aggressive manner.
The skulls are dumb, and who would dare say less?
We throw away a flag to flaunt a banner;
Our caves have echoes which say No to Yes.

In India the smooth sides make one shiver,
But here the walls have teeth, the roof is low;
And suddenly a deep and silent river
Looms out of nothing, and into nothing flows.

Some of the time we walk upright, though slowly,
Often we have to stoop and crouch beneath
A craggy corridor, where aching, lowly,
We reach a cavern strewn with ancient teeth.

And when we reach the light – bare veld and boulder
Hard as the hidden bones within the caves
Stand in the wind, that wind which, growing colder,
Will blow us to the kingdom of shared graves.

IT IS BETTER TO BE TOGETHER

It is better to be
Together. Tossed together
In a white wave, than to see
The ocean like an eagle.

It is better to lie
In the stormy seething
Than to judge the weather
In an eagle's eye.

Cold is the bird
Who flies too far
In the clear vision
Which saints and eagles share:
Their faraway eyes are bitter
With darkened prayer.

O, it is better to try
With the white wave, together
To overturn the sky.

CYCLE

5

Cover my eyes with your palm,
Your darkness is too bright.
One cannot douse in the dark
Such pure, engrossing light.

Marsh-flickering, it flares
In the darkest places;
Aurora-flashing, soars
From a hundred faces,

Who, each one, is now balanced
In the huge extension
To be worthy, challenged
By your glimpse of heaven

Which was so valid, the blind
Hands of darkness seemed
White in your guiding hand,
Bright in your valiant dream.

O cover each heart with your palm.
The brightness that was too bright
Shall make even the Darkness learn
Your pure, engrossing light.

6

The dropped leaf
Held the colour of flame
When the trees stirred.

Now lips cannot shape –
Such winter is grief –
The encompassing word.

The flat seconds pass
In a listless drought,
Unblessed by rain,

And poverty of my mouth
Struggles to form the vast
Two syllables of your name.

7

To eat pain like bread is a condition
A part of living
Which is the condition of dying;
But how slowly. The delicate tissue
Fails where it is fronded; how slowly.

We have a shell light as cocoon, internal
Within which you beat like a promise.

There was a sort of heaven in all you failed
To see, yet saw: that which was hidden
Apt to the touch. The secret garden
With dreaming effacement fashioned
For heroes; brain and heart beating purely
In the old man like a child, and in the child
Beating like age.

Finding music in counterpoint of worlds
In shapes as old as rock, you took the star
In your fingers and drew it over the strings,
Listening with passion to the murmur
That leaps from the secrets of the great man, deaf.
Two hundred of you sang in the Messiah.

In the centuries back of the questioning, you met,
Parted and met, in aloneness, no ears hearing together,
No eyes seeing the same.
Yet you saw: rhythm and speech of harmony
In a statue with loops of nothing, a circle of air.
Statement of colour on colour which, each misreading,
Read purely, if intention is a grace:
Spread in patterns of brightness, later in patterns
Of doom-knowing darkness like a circle of nothing
On circles of water.

Water flows forward and backward. You followed after.
Time was a stream in the spiral, a rock in the stream.
Together we followed the path which distorted, eluded.
How could it not, if the answer sought was the one
Significant beyond measure?

All the majestic vistas – you ventured down all,
Retaining the dream and the laughter. How else be fashioned
So wholly: laughter ringing the bells in my breast?

You were not good to the poor: You enriched them
With eyes and hands that knew to speak and be silent.
You were not kind to the maimed: You unmaimed them.

Remembered now by the nameless servant,
The old man fishing, the singers and doers,
The raucous young voices who fling and linger on areas
Filled with your presence.

But to eat bread like pain.
To eat pain like bread.
To wake in the morning in sunlight
Warm in the sun on the floor
And know with the only real knowledge
Complete, undivided, undoubted,
That your voice will not open the door
Your hand will not latch on the sunlight
Your footstep not ring through the dark.
Ah, Greek with the visage of horror
How can you bear it, the stopping?
How can we bear it, the cruel
Cut of the skein in the morning?

But the morning is you, and the bread
Warm from the oven; the stars
Crammed in your pocket; the singing
Hallelujahs of dreams.

To eat pain like bread is a condition
Of living, which is endless dying.
You will not allow me to refuse
My daily bread.

PHYLLIS HARING

―――

OVERTURE TO STRANGERS

I have seen the light coming up over the town, like ash,
Like the grey wash used by sombre artists, or like a wave
Very slow in arriving when I'm alone on a beach at dawn –
When the print of feet is forgotten and the sand
Lies like a wet yellow handkerchief, sodden with tears.

And ships come and go, in magnificence,
Looming up close to the shore, without lights or sailors.
– The air weeps with salt, and at a certain hour
I turn my back on the sea and my face towards the houses.
And I and workmen with grey faces pass each other
      continually,
They with their grimy lunch-boxes and flasks of tea
And I with my hands empty and nervous, and I move
Constructed with girders of ice, or of glass,
With a high heart towards the inevitable doom and change.

. . . The smell of woodsmoke, of wet plants, of rain
Falling perpetually onto my head; the unreality
Of my friends; follows me, pursues me everywhere.
Believe me when I tell you these things!
That the confused colouring of copper, of cold,
Of Chrysanthemums, continually come to disturb me –
To drown whatever I know in purple seas of negation.

And this is why, along these blank shores,
I wander towards you across the world . . .
While the sea-wash walks with wet feet over my tracks
So that nothing remains of me but eventually perhaps
A pebble, rolling in my skull, idly, falling dully upon

The ivory of teeth smiling forever at the fear of tides.
– I will certainly come to this, my head a hollow cave
For tides; a goblet of bone; a clever castanet;
Or a calabash of teeth and dry weed and whispers.

JUNGLE

We have come to the jungle
And now walk forever in the dark circle
All lost travellers know –
Mocked from the trees by families of idiots,
Where life is a listless looking-for-fleas
And God a giant gorilla feared by all.

Even the orchid we see is dangerous

And faith is the folded wing of vulture
Aware of the doom of jungle;
Hope is the snout of crocodile
Floating in the doom of jungle.
Charity is hyenas' spoil
Rotting in the doom of jungle.

And turning ape, we cry and cling together,
Yammering fearfully at the sound of drums.

THE FORBIDDEN

The juice of apples climbs in me
Along arterial avenues – and it might be
The earth is an apple hanging aimlessly
In air, or fixed forever in some intricate
Astrologer's design, forbidden and sinful
And therefore sorrowful. But my legs

Dominate the earth, performing the magic
Of movement and direction, in love
Lying ridiculously in childish attitudes;
And they fulfil themselves in ankles and feet,
In arteries and knees and the fine bones of feet.
– Even my arms are purposeful, perhaps remorseless
Because of the near smell of apples . . .
The crisp crunch of their beautiful new skins,
Their flesh folding away in the dark of my mouth,
And I must ever and ever return to the tree.
The eyes of the serpent do not persuade me –
The sweet blood of apples beats in my blood.
And yet I am not sustained –
I am not able to go about quietly: this juice
Climbing the tree of me
Gives an autumnal fragrance to my hair,
But my head's a cracking seed which will not grow.

THE EARTH ASKS AND RECEIVES RAIN

The earth asks and receives rain, the benediction
Of rain and of sun, and the population of seeds.
But the worm inhabits the earth, the cadaver
Under the earth, and multiplies itself
And makes merry in the blind earth above which
The birds suspend themselves, aware of the end.

I have walked from one town to the next,
From one village to another, among markets
And harbours, among old men and sailors,
Enquiring the whereabouts of my brother.
I sit in the houses of the people
When there is thunder on the air: the husband
Is home, the children are noisy about the house,
And the woman is weeping over onions, or bad news,
With rain, or perhaps pigeons, skidding on the roof.

And my brother is not the husband of the house,
Nor the child, but I will stay here a little time
For these remind me of my brother.
And the neighbours come and go, with talking
And laughter, surrounded by dogs and by children;
And the earth presses upward against their feet
So that they remain upright: but elsewhere
The earth opens and engulfs a city, and perhaps
My brother is hastening towards that city.

While I, as I lie on my comfortable bed, as the blood
Courses through my hands and my feet, as the blood
Courses over streets and over flagstones, up to the doors
Of houses and cathedrals, over the altars
Of the new religions, over the world, I thrust my thought
Deep into the earth, watching the worm with my mind's eye:
The worm which devours itself with the beak of a dead bird.

FOETUS

Submerged, silent, rooted in water,
My eyes are those of a merchild, stung with salt.
And bones form themselves quietly,
Turned on a lathe of tide . . .
My webbed hands and my feet float and fall,
As I revolve disconsolate in an opaque dreaming.

There is slime everywhere.
There are fishes, and powerful anemones,
And an army of snails softly advancing . . .
Chrysanthemums
Spread themselves on my face and my neck, like fungi,
And my skin crawls, my hands clutch and clasp
The warm temperature of the water.

My head leans on the water, sad as a bell,
Surrounded with silence, with heaviness . . .
Therefore my arms cross my heart
And with humility I hope to die.

TWIN

To make a resurrection there must be a death –
And I have seen the images of love indeed
Attending funerals, ascending in a breath
Of purest smoke; yet also weeping while we read
The service to our self. These are the eyes
Of images, but who is it who dies?

To make a death there must be love to resurrect,
And I have seen the images of death indeed
Approach our life, approach and weep and genuflect . . .
So do the funerals of love and hate proceed:
One is the other, neither what it seems,
Yet one exempts, and one of these redeems.

DAVID WRIGHT

FROM SEVEN SOUTH AFRICAN POEMS

III

My grandfather was an elegant gentleman
Who trod behind an ox-wagon's wheels in his youth
Four hundred miles to Kimberley from Port Elizabeth,
To resuscitate the family fortune.

His love affair with money lasted a long time.
In my childhood I best remember
His glass-panelled car and European chauffeur,
And dignity in a cricket pavilion;

Or when in gardens imitating England
He in a morning-coat between two ladies
Walked. I was afraid to recognize
My father's father, and kept my distance.

Nothing became my grandfather so much as his age.
Impoverished and living in a single room,
He kept his grace and distinguished costume,
Imposing on distress an unstooping carriage.

The lady left him, but he took his congé
Like a gentleman. The old colonial
Never allowed a merely personal
Regret pour a poison in the ear of memory.

VI
For Roy Campbell

My countryman, the poet, wears a Stetson;
He can count his enemies, but not his friends,
A retired soldier living in Kensington,
Who limps along the Church Street to the Swan.

Horses and bulls, the sable and impala,
Sparkle between his fingers, and a sun
That sleeps and rises from the Indian Ocean
Gongs the images of his passion.

He never loved liberty for her name,
Or wept on the disastrous ashes of Guernica,
But he fought for her where he could find her,
Knowing she was not lying in a newspaper column,

But bound, still bound in the aboriginal fall
From Eden and of Adam. His ancestors who came
Out of the eighteenth century and Scotland
Taught him to have no truck with the liberal.

Horses and bulls, the sable and impala,
Thunder between his fingers; as they run,
He hears another thunder in the sun,
Time and the sea about Tristan da Cunha.

FROM SOUTH AFRICAN BROADSHEETS
VIII

Under the African lintel, Table Mountain,
The violet ship at the quay
Casts off, the laughing sentimentalists hold her
Momentarily with coloured streamers
As she moves out to sea.
The paper ribbons part and flutter; and the crowd
Puts forth its handkerchiefs like leaves.

The African continent leans against the peninsula.
In hallways at Kalk Bay
Fishing tackle waits beside a salt-stained surf-board;
The electric trains flicker by
Washed colonial gables, rain-weary oakwoods,
And expensive small hotels,
Stucco villas elbowing for maritime vistas.

O spectacular home of mediocre visionaries
The mailboat draws away
From one of the more terrifying middleclass paradises
Of the shut mind and eye.
I wave from the deck of the Union-Castle liner,
And an exile waves from the quay.
Why do we love the places we were born in?

MORAL STORY II

I met Poetry, an old prostitute walking
Along Piccadilly, one whom one could buy,
Just a draggletail bitch with padding for each breast –
No wonder the corner boys were gay and joking!
She'd laid on paint too thick in a colour too high,
And scuttled like a red hen deprived of its nest.

But she stopped for a word with me, one of her pimps,
Her faithful old ponce still hoping for his percent.
When I asked, 'How's business?' she shook her leary head:
'In peacetime the boys are not so keen on the nymphs;
And I'm getting a bit behind with the rent.
These days the pickings are small that fall from my bed.'

'Wartime was whoretime! Never mind, cheer up, lovey;
Find me another fee like the one from New York:
They pay very nicely, the Yanks – and don't look glum.
– Or go get another girl, if you want more gravy!'
She screamed, '– you've got your good looks yet – or you
  could work!
'Go get yourself a job licking somebody's bum!'

But out of the corner of my eye I'd seen a Rolls Royce
Purr by us with a back seat full of her old friends,
Passing, like the gent in the song, the girl they'd ruined.
They lifted a disdainful nostril at her noise,
And continued as you might expect, to pursue their ends,
With cigars drawing, and the radio carefully tuned

To a highbrow programme. So across the gutter
We caught one another's look; and as their exhaust
Echoed outside the Ritz like a burst paper bag,
Laughed like hyenas; she, with a shaking udder,
Said, 'I was a lovely piece, when they met me first!'
And the lineaments of desire lit the old hag.

F. D. SINCLAIR

ZIMBABWE

Stranger walls, that shell no violent presence,
No mask of gold, no bee-swarm in the skull,

Stand waiting, quietly, without impatience,
Their hour of mortal birth within a mind

That will exalt them in its running vision
From ruin to reality in song.

Here the sea is grass, and here its waves
Are restless hills of grass that surge to hide

What pinnacle of urgent mystery,
Serenely islanded, lies charted still

Within the eye, upon the mind's close map,
Washed by the peaceful tides of day and year.

There is no face beneath the broken stones,
No searching of decay to bring the heart

Nearer to history of blood, and cut
The desolation spun, without, within;

Only silent emptiness of wind
That covers time and crumbles down the walls.

This is a temple that has lost its god
And lies, memorial to solitude,

Fit for re-dedication in the mind
That gives it now a meaning and a song,

Identity from timeless non-existence,
Deeper than thought, earthed in the feeling heart.

ANNE WELSH

WATERFALL

To reach it
Meant going down –
Leaving unfolded silk of sun
For moving shade
Of water and of rock.

This early place,
As secret as the heart,
Where life vibrated
Out of shining centre,
Clothed me again in green
Once I had stripped and shivered
And plunged in.

And crawling, hands and knees,
Over the sharp surfaces
To that safe place
Between the ravaged face
And silver fall,
I was so washed and blinded,
So bludgeoned down by water,
That life could stir in me
Like first free laughter.

SHARPEVILLE INQUIRY

Outside the courtroom
Winter sun is warm.
The streets are quiet,
A child comes out of school –

Hate is on exhibition
Inside that room;
And at the outside tap
A black servant rinses a teapot.

Hate is stripped to its lean
Dead trunk by a winter of words.
It stands nakedly
In the public gardens.

And between the curled contempt
Of the 'public' benches
The line of suffering is growing.
The bright sun sharpens it.

BETWEEN SEASONS

Across this dream of seas blue mountains fall
And light as birds the rocks ride on the waves,
Held in the crook of wings green valleys lie,
And fig trees climb to sun above the caves.

In this wild weather loving crosses over,
Leaving the sparkless sand of this pale shore
To reach another earth, bright cups of fire
The red walled cloisters birds are making for.

There red-winged starlings, bronzed like autumn leaves,
Lift still earth heavenwards in rolls of flight,
And trumpetless, have raised their murmurings
Out of the forest dark to open light.

Oh seas and seasons, none of them complete;
Look how this bursting precipice of black
Throws out the silver missiles of its fish
To be a thousand suns in one attack.

Now into fireless seasons brightness breaks,
Under the blackened strata red cores glow,
Till mystified the sleeping birds will wake.
Between-the-season rain will come and go.

Again these cancelled seasons shall return
And carry burnt-out branches into spring,
Pale colours shall encircle them, and light
Fall accurately on the dark they bring.

And here, within the here, where lank birds scream
And several hollows join between the bones,
Those sheltered valleys and those sun-bright hills
Will join to ours, make light our lightless stones.

THAT WAY

That way. He went that way.
The pink road through the brown hills,
The path across the yellow grass
Towards that lifted place
In those stone folds.

Bleak, they say,
The wind that has no caress
But strips and burns.

The journey will be dusty,
Footfall after footfall.
And first the ash of evening
Will put out colour
Then nightfall overtake him.
The going is blind at times
For rock engulfs.

Moments of shelter,
And of peace, perhaps –
When torn land is consoled,
The broken earth grows whole
And hills are loved by light.

Those coming back?
It's difficult to say –
Worn by weather,
Exposure under stars.

But that rock marks. It makes.
They look the same but have a different shape.
They say, when nothing is withheld
Rock takes them on,
Takes over, gives itself.
They say that terror goes,
That after night,
The shining of the morning is most marvellous.

MANY BIRDS

The travelling eye has seen its many birds.
Quick wings caught
In first unbroken light
Related earth to sky;
Showered up in living sparks
Bursting lit-lifted from the heart of rocks;
Harboured the blue movements of the shade
Within the rings of sun.

Dancing on rock and river
Light's flight is a shiver of touch
And trees with blazing crests
Are raised out of dark roots.
Light lifts in stone and mud,
Rises red-winged in the blood.

The travelling eye has seen its many birds,
Turned to the fleeting focuses
For a stilled time;
Seen the pale passage of the herons homing,
Drop of the brown bird to the brown river.

And travelling under light
Eye sees the birds of light
Shaking and glancing, circling
The still circle and the tree alight
And always moving out of recalling.

Out of light's world, world alight,
Is the still of light.
In the stillness of shining the first morning,
In cessation of movement
The wing's curving.
And in the changing,
In the moments of sleeping and waking,
Light moves in the darkness of loving.

Here is the morning and the evening;
Here red-wings from the hills' warm stones
Are lifted into the blue lightning,
And rivers of sand run
Into the contours of great waters,
And colour is a multiple brilliance.
Here the warm and the dark and the pale
Have burst into one flame
And the fleeting is gathered into the glory.

ROY MACNAB

SEVEN OF THE CLOCK

Seven of the clock and the day
Clean as a copybook, white
As I whistling go on my way,

Two flying feet
Hopscotch through the street
All the way down
To the end of the town,

O breathless I am and blowing
Like a whale, a spinnaker sail
On a Summer sea,

Feet and fist
Reach out through the mist
For the bridge that grows like a Roman nose
In a landscape as noble as this,

Now over I go but adagio
For this is the slow
Movement of Matins,

See far below
The ballet begins
And I make my bow
To swans on a lake,

O this is the hour when life's begun
To unfold in the flower
Face and hands to the sun,

This is the time for the hare to run
From shouts and shadows and
Shots from a gun,

When the stag in the park
Awoke with a start, antlers
Caught in the arms of an oak,

And everywhere suddenly broke
News of a day, bells and chimes
And the definite stroke

Of Seven of the Clock.

MAJUBA HILL

On the craggy mountain-top the mist
Held a redcoat army in its fist.
Beaten by arrogance and the sun,
They dragged their last uncaptured gun
To make a fortress of the hill
And watch all night from the citadel.

The creatures of the mist the sheep
Sniffed round the red men in their sleep,
The only sentries still awake
Who heard the yielding branches break,

For the five-day-sleepless sentry stood
And snored at his post above the wood,
While down upon the stirring plain
The night brought up its Dunsinane.

The moon went skulking from the sky
And hid its face as the wood passed by,
A few score Boer and bearded trees,
Scaling the mountain on their knees.

The dawn rose up from an angry bed,
Drew back the shroud from the mountain-head,
And sent the sun out over the stones
To gnaw at the sleeping soldiers' bones.

The soldiers sleeping in the sun,
Could never know what the night had done,
How bitter were the blazing noons,
The defeat in dust of proud dragoons;
Only the nibbling goat and the sheep
Saw how remote were the dead asleep.

THE ROAD TO BOLOGNA

Castiglione has many a frontier.

The white five hundred and five
Eyes of Christ on the warm hillside
Are blinding in Bologna's light.

Marble and Brescia stone
Shackle an anchor to our load,
And distant as Damascus now
Bologna and our private road.

High in the blazing Apennines,
Before the forest's grasping cone,
The sword embedded in the cross
Sings of a sacrifice in stone,
Permanent as del Robbia sky,
And singing it centres
The century's wrong
Nails my conscience
To its song.

O Paul, Paul ons dood lê hier
Onder die grond se skaduwee,
Stand unshod on their mountain bier,
Salute the symbol of the tree.

So we come to our first frontier;
The cemetery looms like a customs shed,
Have I anything to declare
To the marshalled dead?

EL ALAMEIN REVISITED

Only the sand, only the sand
Caresses them;
Only the wind in its prayers
Sings a requiem.

These whom we left here,
Like sprawled sleepers in the stalls,
When the play is ended
And no attendant calls,

They had not come seeking
'Some corner of a foreign field'
To build a bold heroic pose
With painted letters on a shield

For them there was no questioning
A dry season of twenty years;
They only accepted the desert
And the short salvation of tears.

Theirs was an army without banners;
They paraded no platitudes for fools,
They looked without passion on the cold, grey tanks
And fashioned their deaths with these tools.

Yesterday's hostages born in a cage,
They learnt only the ways of the frail,
And theirs was a road of continuing pain;
Let the years bring comfort, the wind have its tale.

Six feet is no depth for tragic men
Said the wind and the wind never ceases
To pile up high the soft grey tombs,
And move them where it pleases,

Piling the sand-dunes, piling high
Over the desert where the dead men lie,
Up and down against the sky,
Up and down against the sky,

. . . only the sand and wind forget to die.

THE RIVER

The river used to store up in its mouth,
Like betel nut, the red earth plunder of the north,
Beyond the desperate sand-bank's thunder, the current
South from Mozambique blew hot and cold
To break its nerve, the pressure grew
Unbearably, one morning early, roused by the Hindu
Temple bell, we heard the river roar
To its death trampled in the bloody miles of sea.

LAURENCE LERNER

14 JULY 1956

The rockets bubble upward and explode;
The colours scale the slopes of sky and fall.
A few look up; somebody says 'That's all';
No sigh or shudder rises from the crowd.
They must be here because they want to be.

We chatter to the crowd in French and nods;
Shake hands, and pick up children; claim that we
Are also equal, free and brotherly.
The troubled sky suggests the wrath of gods.
'Always the same,' a woman says, and goes.

The fireworks scatter to the ground and die:
Just as the conscript gazers, each one knows,
Might parachute upon their gazing foes:
Invaders from a foreign century.
I hear a whisper scratching at my ear –

An ancient hag drew back her lips to breathe
Her ecstasy upon the festive air.
She might well be the oldest woman there
– Or so the concentration in her teeth
And damp absorption in her eyes suggest.

A wisp of gesture spirals from her wrist
Towards the crimson sky. The oldest there?
The sky turns gold. I wonder if for her
Algeria or 'eighty-nine exist.
The fading sparks find mirrors in her eyes.

Who are the fireworks for? Old hags, old men,
Children up late, and straggling foreigners?
No-one is old enough to know the cause,
Or young enough to feel he is not in
A troubled crowd beneath a troubled sky.

ST ENDA

He stood upon the coast of County Clare.
The grey mist rising from the freckled sea,
And saw the misty islands. 'Who lives there?'
'They make their soil of seaweed; not a tree
Grows on that land where God left all things bare.'

He went, and stayed. Perhaps he'd have preferred
An uninhabited and holier isle.
Occasionally the king his brother heard,
From islanders who came for turf or oil
And stayed for Mass, how well he preached the Word.

Then others followed, hearing of his fame.
Enda was pleased at first: his work was sped:
Especially when the seven Romans came.
All Europe knows the isle of saints, they said,
And promised that the Pope would hear his name.

But they all stayed on Aran, and died there.
He told no-one how bad that made him feel.
He tired of books, and work, and even prayer:
Perhaps he should have found a barren isle.
He gazed across the sea at County Clare,

Or climbed the heights above Killeany Bay
To see the ancient fort, or look out west
Across the freckled sea. He sat all day,
Too tired to think. The brothers were impressed:
'He is so holy he can only pray.'

The Pope did hear: but Enda never knew.
Vaguely he sensed his power rested on
His wish to give it up: what could he do?
Cairan and Breacan saw the work got done;
The more he hated fame, the more it grew.

A kind of wisdom came when finally
He'd grown too holy to believe in God:
All that you want you get eventually
If you no longer want it. So he died,
Old and unhappy, gazing out to sea.

Note: St Enda brought Christianity to the Aran Islands in the
fifth century. He died on Innishmore, the largest island, which
later became known as the Island of Saints.

THE POET AT FIFTY

'And would you sign my copy sir?' 'A Scotch?'
'Which of the younger poets do you admire?'
('A snooty bastard and he drinks too much').
He hardly answers while the young men stare,
Misquote his lines, and pester him with praise.
Far back behind his eyes
A ghost slips off,
Seeks to avoid the light and wanders, lost,
Within the spreading thicket of the past.

His greying hair is longer now than when
He'd bang the table till the glasses swayed
And beer like talk went splashing through his brain.
He'd speak his measured words across the air,
Or thinking of the future sit and stare,
Watching the puddles cross the table top,
Watching them creep and stray, and as they spread
Falter, and frothing stop.

And now he hacks out words from memory,
Hides in the thicket, sips his Scotch, and finds
Obliterated paths to stumble by
Into the mess of leaves and mud, and there,
Tearing himself on brambles, looking for
That secret clearing where the ground is dry,
Dreams of the swathing darkness where he'll lie.
As murmurs straggle dimly from the light:
'What are you writing now?' they ask, polite.
He hears it all; awakes; his feet are wet.
He hates it when they call him sir; and yet
Is angry when they don't.

He hates the causes that have failed, he hates
The present for succeeding to the past;
He hates that youngster who appreciates
His poems and why he wrote them; and at last,
Emerging from the thicket, comes to know
How much he hates the world he lives among,
Bewildered by the gay unmeasured flow
Of chatter from the reasonable young
Who love each other so.

ALL DAY AND ALL OCTOBER

All day and all October
I watched the great lime sway,
Sat indoors and shivered,
Watching the wind all day:
Seeing the past reflected in
The tumble down the window pane.

While the season fingered
With the half-clad tree,
Leaf on leaf the present
Dropped into memory:
Lusting for the past I stood
And in my sight the summer died.

As Winter like a lecher
Stripped the branches bare
The shape of last October
Stood on the naked air:
The glass keeps out what time is at;
The dead leaves die like years, and rot.

The wordless wind of winter
Set this great lime going
(I sit and count the years)
Will knock it down one day
(And in my tumbling tears
The pain of knowing):
I and my wordy lust
Long since away.

YEARS LATER

They tied my mother's legs when I was born.

You ask my sister: she must know it all,
She must remember.
                    Eighteen years ago
They tied my mother's legs with her own shawl.

I felt their laughter shaking in her blood.
That was my world before I felt the world,
Their booted laughter washed through waves of blood.

They laughed, and tied her legs: they always did.

I felt her shuddering as I beat my head
Against the bone, withdrew, then beat again,
Again, and then again: my splintering skull
Trying to find the mouth that led to air
And to the sounds of laughter:

                          tight as teeth
The lips were pressed, and still I beat, and still,
Feeling her screams like splashes in the tide
That took me in its rhythms up to where
The world began, and tight lips turned me back.
There was no world: only those twisting tides,
The choking blood, my torn and twisted head,
The dying sound of laughter in the dark.

My sister got away five years before.
Tonight she dozes at the kitchen fire,
Her husband out, the children all in bed
(Easy she bore them, at nine pounds a head)
And dreams in German (half-forgotten now)
Of me, and mother (whom she hardly knew),
Of all our deaths, and of six million more.
The flames leap softly in the roaring fire.

For months on end she never thinks of it.
After the war she read the books on what
The Allies found – the dead, the worse than dead.
She read the papers till her eyes were red:
She read them like an ally – pitied us,
Tried to imagine the inhuman mess,
And failed, and tried, imagining the guilt,
The pain, the beatings she had never felt,
The treacheries, the horrors that were told.

The war began when she was eight years old.
She was the lucky one, she got away,
Outlived us all; the memories that lay
Below her life lay still and did not wake.
Now she is thirty, married, lives in York.
Her sons are young, she's told them nothing yet.
'They'll learn; the world is wicked; let them wait.'

So why, tonight, should she remember me
And feel our mother's shudders through her limbs,
Our mother's screams possess her silently?
Something is rasping in her mouth, like grit,
A dirty finger foraging among
Her gums, a slug squeezed flat against her tongue,
An oily rag entangled with her spit.

I taste like grit and oil against her lips:
She feels me kick, she feels her membranes torn;
She shuts her teeth to keep the surge of blood
From bursting out, she shuts her lips as though
They were the helpless lips that long ago
Kept me from being born.

EARTH, SKY

I walked with a flower
Stuck red in my coat.
It flamed for an hour
And then it went out.
The hilltop above me
Shimmered like stars;
The houses passed me,
They were white upon white.
Then the dark came around.
I thought of my child,
His body a flower,
His heart like a star;
And the dark came around.

I put down the flower
And I walked on my way –
It is surely there still
But not as a flower.
And I thought of my child
Who has come from the dark:
From night of the sky,
From deep of the ground;
And I thought of my child
Till the sun came around,
Till the sun came around.

THE SLEEPER

(*For Marge*)

When you awake
Gesture will waken
To decisive things.
Asleep, you have taken
Motion and tenderly laid it within,
Deeply within you.
Your shoulders are shining
With your own clear light.
I should be mistaken
To touch you even softly,
To disturb your bold
And entirely personal devotion
To the self that sleeps
And is your very self,
Crucial as when you hasten
In the house and hasten through the street,
Or sit in the deep yellow chair
And breathe sweet air.

Unaware of the stars
Outside our window
That do not know they shine,
As well as of the wild sea
That can have no care,
As well as of the wind
That blows unaware
Of its motion in the air,
Sound be your rest
And gentle the dreaming
Of your silent body
Passionately asleep.
Can a cloud stay so still?
Can a bird be so lonely?

It seems you have found
Great patience in your breath:
It moves with life,
It rehearses death.

THE SEA AND THE EAGLE

The sea contains a destiny,
Also the broadwinged eagle.
Both with an equal loneliness
Devour their continents.

Bird, where are you bound,
Borne on the surfs of height?
There is nothing unknown in the air.
Why do your wings flow up and upward?

Whose silence, waters, and what wound
Do you conceal in thunder?
Your beak has worried the bones of earth
Longer than the seasons have been about
Our robes, rising and falling,
And mingling us in the flowing metre.

We have given you both a mystery.
Reveal it and we shall see ourselves
Suddenly like a rising wing,
Terribly like a swoop of water.

THE GRAVE'S CHERUB

So wild yet candle-calm
He lifts his sword of stone,
And stress of his marble eyes
Staring for paradise.

Homeless head he raises,
His small right hand supplants
The thought of peace:
Clenched in the light of the land,
A tragic actor's hand.

All night long,
All daytime, stares
In the moon and the sun,
Through summer and through winter airs,

His pitiless angelic face,
Eyes fixed hard on the living
Who eat their pain like bread.
Some mourners come,
Bringing bright flowers for the dead.

Fresh gusts of the wind
Reverse the sharp leaves.
The mind blown back,
Each mourner grieves.

In the broad wingfolded
Wingbeating place:
Orbit of stillness,
Sundazzled meeting-ground
Of human and angel face.

POETRY IS DEATH CAST OUT

Poetry is death cast out,
Though it gives one chance to retaliate.
Death takes it but the poem moves
A little further beyond death's gate;

153

And I know the proof of this. Once walking
Amongst bushes and lizard stones I found
A little further than I had thought
To go, a stream with a singing sound.

ANIMAL KINGDOM

Spading earth
I thought of the earth. Here
and there gazelle and hog
locust and elephant
fly and frog
collecting their light, leapt
frumped pondered and whizzed
and the river that I heard
included birdsong.

What happens when the sun
dewed with such joy, shines on, spills down
on gazelle and hog
locust and elephant
fly and frog
pond hand stalk and loquat
river and beak?

I want I have I give I love
I answer the senior core of the sun
I speed the body of the warm gazelle
I lift the elephant high in my thought
like a cloud of heaven that moves so slow
and the fly I follow, the dustheap find
my plumtree grows from a clod of sleep.
Locust locust leap with me
water flow and mirror me.

DAWN HIPPO

The size of a cavern for men to crouch in
by fire trickling small;
for demons uttered by name
to crowd like tropical thunder
and crackle against the wall,

he domes the birth of day:
built moving on the river,
shrubless mound of weighty sheen,
a large derisive slope
hammering back each ray,
he floats his quiet hilltop,
he sizes up the morning;
a zone of bubbles happens round his head,
streaks of his glitter spear them dead,
breaking the break of day.

A fine froth scums his sides like primitive acid,
birds with sharp beaks fly over him;
he bulges landward
choosing a shelved approach.
The water shallows where he wants it to,
pushes in savage rings that smash
high reeds and rock the river. Mud swarms,
mud slimes his paddling belly as he climbs,
heavily wagging the water away.
The full ridiculous splendour mobs the stones.
Thunder and lightning jostle on his bones.

PRINCE HENRY THE NAVIGATOR

I

The Navigator

At the summit of perception
a blackness starts to rise:
raw images of darkness
unkempt alarming skies

that can torment the sturdy mind
to grief or shibboleth.
Day's daylight is the reckoned tune,
night's huge and driving breath

ordains the heart of knowledge,
the spokes that spin the wheel,
the meditating lantern,
the star-revolving keel.

2

Meditation on dry land

Through the leafy Lisbon trees I heard
the frogless ocean whiten wild as flutes.

When I wandered in Lisbon's blossoming darkness
or sat in my house, suddenly afraid

of winged horizons perched on the prow,
strange and pure their dome of singing,

silent I prayed, my task began.
I cross the deliberate gulf of man.

D. A. GREIG

TO A FLEA IN A GLASS OF WATER

I caught you grazing on my knee
And dropped you here. You think I'm God?
Presume my 'broad humanity' –
I'll let you sink, gorged with my blood.

Why should I save you, airborne itch?
You think your leapers limp as thread,
And helpless, make my conscience twitch?
It's death that keeps our history fed,

And books are filled with better deaths
Than yours, and God himself took lives
For less offence and stopped up breaths
For less rebellion than your knives.

You think your primitive despair
Will draft my city conscience? No,
These streetlamps hook in Absalom's hair,
On pavements Saul and David go.

ON A SCOOTER

The sun's low light splinters in a plastic gleam
Of goggles as she rounds the bend,
My Vespa virgin in a mechanistic dream
Perhaps of flowers, macadam without end,
Perhaps just listening to the tiny roar
Caged frettingly between her knees:
Her head floats in a mirador
Among glowing grass, she and it a tease
Of which is which, all dazed with sun –
Or is it me that blends them all together
Until her floating hair is one
With the grasses' dazzled feather?
I stand, I wake (so afternoon beguiles),
Up to the kerb she comes; she switches off; she smiles.

DOUGLAS LIVINGSTONE

ONE TIME

It seems a certain time ago: a-maybe
seven years or less, he
first took a woman underwater. In aqualungs
and bathing suits, hanging
in the pale liquid air
of a blue cathedral
– the sleeping pool of the limestone caves
to be precise –
face mask to mask,
wide-eyed and glass to glass,
they triumphed over the first knotty cotton fumblings
in the allembracing wetness.

Her hair, like a damp Medusa's,
flared upwards.

He remembers their delight at the silent
new experience,
their emulations of the passions
of dolphins
who are not after all
unhonourable
and very humorous
and humouring in their loveplay.

Then, he recalls his panic
when, with a mounting climax,
perhaps upside down, certainly weightless,
he had to cram her mouthpiece

back into her vacant lips, fishwide and cyanosed,
her eyes lightly closed,
and it was a long swim away
to the surface. (Her hair hung down on the journey.)

She did, of course, recover adequately
after a few splutters and with him gently
squeezing her ribs regularly
while finning desperately
upwards.
        But it was some time
before they tried it again
– some time after
and in shallower water.

PEACE DELEGATE

Tight-sphinctered and inhibited,
  stretching his insteps for stature
  down corridors blank of fixture,
the old gall of last night's defeat

rolling in his mouth like the rust
  of familiar furred and salt stones,
  he arrives stands nods bows coughs frowns,
sits and fiddles with the head-set,

selects a translation, turns low
  the tinny volume and leans back
  from the green baize tables where break
the nations' hearts like billiard play:

the balls softly cannon and click
  wetly. Grey-faced he dreams of limbs
  yellow in bare hotel bedrooms,
cigarette ash on the carpet

and underwear in the closet;
   picks his teeth and sadly reflects
   on futility. He objects,
not often, but when expected –

the futility of nations
   and the dove – grunts alert to hear
   Cannibalism in his good ear,
resettles with shrugged impatience:

the Congo again. He swims gently
   away from fuzzy rhetoric –
   a fly on the ceiling – the click-
snicking cannons on so peacefully.

SUNSTRIKE

A solitary prospector
staggered, locked in a vision
of slate hills that capered
on the molten horizon.

Waterless, he came to where
a river had run, now a band
flowing only in ripples
of white unquenchable sand.

Cursing, he dug sporadically
here, here, as deep as his arm,
and sat quite still, eyes thirstily
incredulous on his palm.

A handful of alluvial
diamonds leered back, and more: mixed
in the scar, glinted globules
of rubies, emeralds, onyx.

And then he was swimming in fire
and drinking, splashing hot halos
of glittering drops at the choir
of assembled carrion crows.

TO A DEAD ELEPHANT

Old Python Nose with the wind-rolling ears:
   Hau! I remember it well when you came,
   thin, small, grey, twinkle-eyed, stumbling and lame,
to me, a lone boy with none of the fears
that stalked the elders. Friend, I had no tears
   for both our young losses; but all the same
   you robbed me of those sweet potatoes!
                           Fame
walked with us, both motherless, those coupled-years.

But who can tame the trumpeter, the hill
   who stands invisible with bright old eyes,
so slow, tree-bulky, dangerous and still?
   Why did you leave me to the elders' lies?
Both men, we meet again, but not my will
   wrought this antheap with flies and hamstrung thighs.

AN EVASION

An old man sits in wrinkled reverie.
A chiselling of violin music at dusk
evokes her, carving her composite husk
hewed from caryatids of his memory.

The blue smoke of the distant fir-clad hills
redolent of pine, marjoram and thyme
brings back her hair like strands of ancient rhyme
blowing over the weathered window sills.

Sometimes, the tired red cobras of her lips
the crests of her teeth, widen, part at him
in false words. Her eyes mock over a rim
of glass, down-lashed, intent on secret sips.

His slim, suntanned dream moves light as moonlight
on water elusive to his slow grasp
as recalled from the time he rose to clasp
her shadowed form from out his shrunken night.

When she fades or will not come, his old dull
eyes film. He becomes aware of the snows
packed around the bottle of his heart and knows
the play of spidery fingers in his skull.

Her inconstancy at first delights and then
enrages him. In the end he forgives
everything. Dozing in the sun, he lives
for her alone; his own kin past his ken.

Another set of eyelids he could drop
behind these outward ones, like a bland shutter
or spades of death emptying earth upon her.
He does not choose to cause her life to stop.

JEAN LIPKIN

PRE DOMINA

Because time kept
From the tip of its tongue
The split-bellow blast
Of ever-lastingness.

Because the kill-tide tarried;
The cut-cross greened
On a filling tree.

While the palm fanned and fattened
Its shadow and fruit
No cellular portent
Warned their root.

Lambs large as flowers
Sashed round in grasses
Belled the hills of Galilee.

While the holy girl
Not yet separate
From the gush and purl of girls
Slept mortal all morning.

FATHER

Lately his haunch has grown stiff
He cannot shift out of his own bent.
The silencer is off his chest.
Wheezing in the acoustic ear
He crackles with static.
His memory veers unchecked
And swerves into old times and places.
Grant to him his fraudulent boast;
In the host of his withering
Let him shiver with pleasure
Recalling the measure of youth's arena.
His tall story is now his truth.
Do not doubt his world however spacious
For it is so, when men go down steeply
The sky grows big.
The sky grows big.

D. R. BEETON

AUTUMN

Patterns of old green-gold trees,
Patterns of aloes dipped in blood;
The khaki veld hums, a long singing
Late-noon dream. And I shall come

Up to the house and its purple shades,
And talk to my father, and he will
Tell me of the world that has been,
And I shall tell him of the world

That will come, and he will tell me
That it is wrong, wrong, and I
Shall think that he is wrong, old and wrong.
But when I emerge into the khaki veld

And feel the fine air stabbing out at me,
And the night that is sweeping up
Across the world, I shall sometimes
Think that he is right, young and right.

G. C. MILLARD

HOSPITAL

We pointed it out to his bed-ridden eyes,
Helping him from the taxi,
A new maternity wing for non-whites;
Black babies, his old whistle of a voice
Made audible, feeding his death-over-there look
With a moment's life;
I'd drown every damn one of them at birth, he said,
And we reached the wheel-chair at the reception.

In the evening we came back, his family,
Half-mingling between beds with other survivors,
Skull on a fresh pillow, breathing,
A kind of father, a kind of husband,
Never loving the telegraph-wires he fixed
For forty years, ending quite suddenly
At midnight, screened with green curtains
From the living.

Cremated decently on a fine morning,
Flowers, coffin of good wood,
Two neighbours, two cronies,
A hired minister.
The Daimler drove us back very slowly;
I changed into shorts at home
And went to Jan Smuts Ground and cricket
To concentrate very hard on strokes and scores
The old man had loved more than he could say.

PATRICK ROLAND

SPRING BURNING

Late in the afternoon;
Before the rain,
Before the summer,
A dead branch bursts –
Blazes at the tip.
A boy runs forward from the men
And dropping flame like seed
Sows the hills with fire.

And when the rain breaks
In the mountains
He will see that flame
Go green through grass,
Grow fat in the bellies of his father's oxen
Grazing, slow and red.

And through his life, his dreams
Fire will be his knowledge:
Will glow there bright in innocence
And burn with fury through his age.

PERSEUS ADAMS

THE WOMAN AND THE ALOE

Although accustomed to picking them, it always
Holds me, makes my spirit draw in its breath
To see their hawk-eyed aristocracy in my house.
Nothing else can so quickly, and with such pure art
Raise up my thorn-riddled love for this place
Hard as banishment – yet lit with wild sweetness too.
A neighbour to stones am I, a sister to a priceless gift.

The prosecuting sun that has one in the witness box
All day, the vastness that is distance gone astray
The koppies thrusting toward heaven
Their blunt, grudging prayers, the small whirlwinds
As if the land were trying to spell out poems
Are all caught, embossed in these firebrands
Stinging me down gauntlets of remembrance.

It was five children and several droughts back
That I came to this farm near Oudtshoorn,
Came city-bred to help build a home
On some tense acres far from my starting ground.
I believed that the fire of the aloe was in me then
But I was mistaken. It was the green blood of youth.
The aloe talks truly only to those who have endured her wait.

Here time has time to make itself felt
And there's no running off to your mother
When trouble coils you in. You might say a mate
And growing children are enough to rock
A woman's demons to sleep, but I tell you here
It's not so, though the silence and loneliness have beaten
The walls of my identity and failed.

At the bend in the tracks the train has a wolf-whistle
For me calling me to return
Where things are gayer and I can be music
And the theatre's guest instead of their outcast whore.
And when the long hands of night reach out
To bless the flowering scrub and my family sleeps
I have called to the past, I have wept at the bitter gate.

And that is why when I look at this fierce plant
My breath catches, a wrapt tenderness falls.
Our kinship carries the undertow of twelve deep
Seasons together; we can die but never mellow
What a bane it must be to the cold heart of Death
That beauty could rise and be stronger than this heat.
A neighbour to stones am I, a sister to a priceless gift.

THE MURDER TRIAL

Being the trial for murder of a young coloured man who
attacked and robbed a white man, here called Mr Fourie

Your shrunken head was bent
But not as it would be
Shortly, on the state's axis of hemp.
Bastard dreamer
Whose life had always hung by a thread
How would one
Betrayal of the floor
Put right the stones with blood on them?

I had not known
The law was such an unrealistic thing,
Pompous, marching mountain
Dressed in a sunset's gown
And served by such absolute gravity
To let your little bones swing:
The moon was on you that night –
You and Mr Fourie.

For six weeks you have sat or stood
While they hooked or quarrelled your drunken act
On to their Ledger page,
For six weeks you have been in your crow's nest
Their look-out, and their prize.
I wonder if my thoughts had an ally
Watching your warm wickedness
Plotted by such cold and cross-word compasses. . . .

A four-letter feeling jerked you into shape
A four-letter caring robbed you of rope,
And deaf ears drummed
Your frail and daggered lightning
Through the ukulele, bandaged dark . . .
When smouldering men light brandy women
The bed-springs murmur of obituaries
And mourning mothers cry out from the cells of stars.

My head has screwed to see
This tennis-match of our failure
I held my heart in my hand
Covered, like the others and dreamt
Of fathers and sons, murderers and daisies,
And then in a dream much older:
When men were fuses that could fire the world
And while I dreamt, the circle grew tighter.

The last day came, dark day of sentence
And the benches garlanded with status.
The judge walked in, the people stood
The judge sat and the people listened
Hearing a widow consoled with additional blood.
Can a trapdoor swallow want
As the grave lets in light?
Black is my cry, black to the roots of sight.

MY GRANDMOTHER

As sinewy as biltong, as narrow
As the path around her house
She keeps her pride intact,
Fiercely erect, with both eyes, her hands, her feet
Her half-blind crooked legs
Intent on the unbending God
Dazing her from above;
The coast she hugs is cruel and comfortless.

Intolerant of so much of
The champing, leering, breath-blown-on-to-old-chafed-
        hands
Snickering world, she keeps a short leash
To her cupped bit, her palms held close
Like a cat on a mat
With a sharp scratch and a bite
For those who love the light
But find the source too cold.

Yet should you be stranded or unaided
Or yield to temptation's bait
Finding no answer from the decentralized
Warmth you feel and covet all about
She will not be gay or quick or glib
But will lead you out
Showing you how strait is the gate
How good the reward.

Being strong, she knows the cold
And fears it. As lonely as a prophet
Her dogma rages unheeded
Binding her motherhood and sealing
The scattered seed: And her house has known
The deafening lights that now stands
Exiled in age and marooned by her convictions,
Its grief beaten into whispers.

172

Only the pupils interrupt her vigil
The unwilling students of her clodhopping
Adopted tongue. How gratefully she goes
Her plough-blades gleaming, towards those morning fields,
Her fixed labours crossing the long afternoon
Till a ripple of wind pushes
The arid windmill far back in her old Dutch veins
And she rises absorbed, her self-hood grinded to a wave of
    light.

Soon, they are gone and her waiting
Resumes. The tall shadows begin their evening task
Of flagging off the jagged
Or unrepentant intruders: The burrows
Are warm and glad about her bones where she tunnels
Deep in her body's mistake: And within she prays
For that abrupt landslide, the huge mountain
Of rectifying darkness, now all but level with her sight.

C. A. FAIR

CHINESE POEMS: ARTHUR WALEY

Rivers that flowed divided each from each,
Hills hid the sky, and all roads led away
Into far lands whose names these poets say:
Separation, absence underlie their speech.

A letter, a flower passed. By snow-bound streams
They paused to write their quiet, resigned, still lines.
The wind breathed longing through the mountain pines;
Their grief rose up to meet them in their dreams.

Shall we do this? We have done all this before,
Have seen ourselves against the frozen scene.
All the sad language of the heart has been
Audible long. We know what is in store.

Like theirs, our future is to mark the road
Bounding our provinces, where mountains rise,
To see how long it is, and where it lies,
And go, though our paths separate for good.

GEOFFREY HARESNAPE

THE AFRICAN TRAMP

He rested in the cool, that traveller.
In the cool world where the tree root curled
He lay upon his face to sleep.

What did he have to say to the little flowers
Grinning wickedly in the grass next to his nose?

First of all he commended them:
'Congratulations, you devils, for keeping up those yellow
        smiles
When everything is blue and windy.'

Then he thought:
'If only I could be fluttering on a stalk like that,
Deep in the green, which shelters so, in the soft wind,
Dreaming above my leaves.'

No, to hell with it!
He didn't want the flowers, he didn't need to worry about
        them,
They looked after themselves, thank God.
All he had to have was a good sleep:
Such a slumber, far, far gone,
With darkness to cradle his brains.

He snuggled into the earth, tried to clasp it,
The sand warm on his arms.
The tree went up next to his head like a pillar,
Creaking as a cage of pine-needles swayed above him.

Lower than the bushes he lay there,
His back-side and shoulders under the grass.
His pepper-corn head was a small, black anthill –
The kind the children kick over in the fields.

But inside his skull was profound, profound,
The wonder-beyond-thought for a man in sleep,
With a few yellow flowers smiling in all that blackness.

In the cool world where the tree root curled,
He lay upon his face asleep.
The sun, the big flower, looked at him through the leaves.

C. J. DRIVER

BIRTHDAYS

Aged twenty-six
I am afraid to die,
That last night's dream
Of an old fat-faced man
Trapped in a war of sweat
Might take my face from me.

Aged twenty-five
I caught a disease
Of each alone in a cage,
Who in goes striding
And out comes crawling
To daily dying flesh.

Aged twenty-four
I saw how hunger
Shoved its thin fingers
Into each skin and eye
Till abstractions lived
In define of bone.

Aged twenty-three
I spoke out bravely,
Named the people's needs –
Declared my private war,
Great abstractions made
Of love and death and pain.

These celebrations of age
Have jumped each fact
With new lust, new flesh –
Till I trouble my bones
With a love each year
And each love a last.

But I am devised
Only a means to die;
What is now, what was,
Must share my cage
With that fat-faced man
Who comes, my age himself.

IN SOLITARY CONFINEMENT, SEA POINT POLICE CELLS

In the early morning
    when the light and the sea smell come stumbling in
        (salt, sea, sun, and the green
            imagined breakers)

I greet the shadows
    with the names of my brothers and sister
        and watch them coil and yawn
            on morning's grey wall.

I breed a new sense
    to learn the secrets known to the sea
        how our drowning flesh dissolves
            until yellow the bones

Go rolling, rolling,
    into generation of sand, shell, and sandstone
        and leave only the rise and the fall of the seas'
            far Atlantic roll.

TO JANN, IN HER ABSENCE

If she asks why the sun
Knocks so loudly at the window,
Tell her nothing but a shadow
Has so much permanence
As love, that has nothing
But doubt to feed on.

If she asks why her love
Speaks so quietly of a closed house
In the city, a window
Where the light cannot come in,
Tell her no-one but traitors
Walk so quietly as love.

These are images I have made
From my loneliness, have carved
From the stone of my country,
Have weaved like blankets
For my sleep. These images
Sing as quietly as love.

STEPHEN GRAY

GIRL WITH DOVES

One dove has its head turned
under a wing, the other is
sort of sitting up in her hand.
I won't look at her face, but
her arms are stretched out just
as if I should take them, and
the doves. This one is so
ready to be taken, and its
companion keeps on sleeping.

Something in her face –
I can't look at the chips off
her nose and the mouth, the
thousands of years between her
and me. And the doves will
suddenly fly out of her hands.

GIRL WITH LONG DARK HAIR

I asked her why she didn't
comb it out,
and she came closer
without answering, wrapped
it over my face until
I knew how dark it was.

BARRY O. HIGGS

PARSON'S PLEASURE

In the vestibule behind the church I saw the parson
And Miss Lizabet
Covertly conspiring
To examine a spider.

In the corner of the vestibule behind the church I saw
The spider wriggling
Down through his long thread
To rear up his head.

I saw the parson pick up the broom to sweep it out
Quietly whispering
To Miss Lizabet
That he would not kill it.

Then I saw Miss Lizabet take hold of the broom and drop it
Sighing confidentially
To the parson perspiring
That God made the spider.

Then she said that if God made the spider in the vestibule
That was where it was meant
To run down its thread
And lift its mighty head.

Then the parson said If that's what it wants to do then
I shall not prevent it.
I did not invent it.
Only God sent it.

After that I left Miss Lizabet and the parson there
Covertly conspiring
To allow the spider
To seek its pleasure.

DEAF

deaf is like
dead I
always think.
not to hear
Some one
call you
back.
Deaf is a stone
to be confused
with not great valleys echoing
or then perhaps
a waving tree
but
doesn't the wild wind
whistle

NIGHT SHORE

I awoke only to hear the dull clobbing of the wind
and the creckling of an ashy log in the fire.
the swabbing of the sea, and saw
its white fingers tremor-taken up the quick sand.
and knowing all was well
I rasped a windy match and shucked a shigarette
and shlopped my head into the billow.

REVERSION

To the wild wild beat of a tom tom tom
I went for a stomp with my honey.
She laughs like a horse and
She stomps like a horse and
She lies on the ground like a sloth sloth sloth
To the grunt grunt grunt of a pig.
She eats her porridge with a wooden spoon
And scratches her bum with the handle
And she sleeps all day to the tune tune tune
Of her glorious glorious snout snout snout
Of her wonderful wonderful snout.

IN LORD CARPENTER'S COUNTRY

Under the slumber and winter of a silent night
The hornblowers of hierarchy on each mount of white

Olives and juniper-berries and ate of steaming bread,
Host of the hornblowing goblet deep as blood.

We had all surfeit of such paltry dishes,
Sausage cabbage and even pottage of fish

Soup red deer's meat and an old waiter
Bearing water, white coat white beard white water.

From there across the wayside with my father
The streetdiggers by the laughing tavern and the carters

Come down, there, all walking with the pipesmoke
Of earlier moon rake, the din that shook

The eaves of the drinking tavern wet as wine
With whiskey, sharp beer and cheers of the flying

Dutchman, so the sparrows of the evening
Spoke also, but nobody bought them a drink.

On, to the main street village, bearing a
Sack of nails for the farrier, where

Burnt gin black vodka and brandy also burnt,
And were comforted hugely by fat Mrs Flaherty.

That was all, save for the nightjar on our soft roof
Dipping his beak in water, my father's friends above

The brawling hill grew silence in my ear;
They know now nothing, but tomorrow will again drink beer.

And yet, there was no dream of pain
On Christmas merry Jesus day.

ANTHONY EATON

THE DOVE APOLOGIZES TO HIS GOD FOR BEING CAUGHT BY A CAT

My lord, I was accustomed to swill about the sky
with speed of my own strength; I swayed
flickering in the sun, I outswerved the hawk,
the trees were gardens of danger and delight for my passing.
I set my wings, and all the world and all
its cloud-companions swivelled with crazy shift –
I was quicker than noon and night,
quicker than my hunters' guns, quicker
than tempest's fist, the universe danced for my mind
and my mind was like a feather on the wind,
gone before they knew it there . . .
I was the master and sole recipient
of all air's system; I ran singing curves
between the marbled clouds. If anything, remember this:
I lived in sunlight, steeply and well.

My lord, forgive me for dying thus. I had forgot
my legs were weak, those of the cat so fast,
and I was in her territory then . . . It seems a final turn of luck
that I should thus go down, that I
who'd scattered the smooth currents of the sky
should end in shower of unseen quills,
and through my own forgetfulness. Think not that I com-
    plain:
rather I marvel that in your scales
a minute's slackened watch should overweigh
and cancel out the hundred million miles of sky and sun.
So all the wondrous tracks of heaven and earth,

of trees and rain, dawn and day's end, wings and the wind,
unite and signify at last
in rotting corpse beside the hedge. My lord,
these words may seem upstart in arrogance; remember
       though,
that with my life you gave me no apology,
and hear them whence they come.

JILL KING

GRIEF PLUCKED ME OUT OF SLEEP

Grief plucked me out of sleep
(for whom? for whom?)
breaking proportions,
narrowing the room

narrowing the room,
widening my heart,
no space for comfort,
no place apart;

widening my heart,
lowering the sky.
In grief's dimension
captive I lie,

all the world's area
shrunk to a room,
my night shaped by grief —
for whom? for whom?

Translations

———

AFRIKAANS SECTION

The following initials indicate the translators:
B. – Guy Butler; C. – Jack Cope; D. – Anthony Delius;
K. – Uys Krige; M. – Ruth Miller; N. – Adèle Naudé;
Ku. – Dr Dan Kunene; Mc. – C. M. Mcanyangwa.

EUGÈNE MARAIS

THE DANCE OF THE RAIN

Song of the fiddler, Jan Konterdans,
from the Kalahari

Oh the dance of our Sister!
First she peeps slily over the mountain top,
  and her eyes are shy;
    and she laughs softly.
And from far off she beckons with one hand;
her armbands flash and her beads glitter;
    softly she calls.

She tells the winds of the dance,
she invites them, for the clearing is wide and it will be a great
      wedding.

The big antelope race up from the plains
  they bunch on the hilltop,
straining wide their nostrils
  and they swallow the wind;
and they bend to see her faint footmarks in the sand.

The little people deep under the ground hear the rustle of
      her feet
  and they creep nearer and sing softly:
    'Our Sister! Our Sister! You have come! You have
      come!'

And her beads shake
and her copper anklets glint in the sloping of the sun.
  On her forehead the fire-plume of the mountain eagle;
    she steps down from the heights;
  she spreads out the grey kaross with both her arms;
    the breath of the wind is lost.
    Oh, the dance of our sister!

C., K

THE DESERT LARK

Song of Nampti, the little Bushman girl

GAMPTA, my little grey sister,
all that I have in the world
  beside my old grandmother!
When you sing up in the sky
  you can see all the wonderful things below;
    the hare creeping away
    and the little steenbuck making its lair.
And the young girls cannot harm you
  for you are stronger than all
  though you are weaker than I.

Even the mountain lion, whose roaring
  scares us at night
    cannot touch you.
I shall watch over you, my sister,
  till all your nestlings are grown.
    My little grey sister, Gampta,
      I see you!

K., C.

THE SORCERESS

Song of the exiled young woman

What becomes of the girl who lives always alone?
She no longer waits for the hunters to come home;
she no longer builds a fire of blackthorn wood.
   The wind blows past her ears;
she no longer hears the dancing song;
   the voice of the story-teller is dead.
No-one calls her from afar
   to speak fine words to her.
All she hears is the voice of the wind alone
   and the wind mourns always
     at being alone.

C., K.

HEART-OF-THE-DAYBREAK

Song of the Desert Lark interpreted by the little Bushman girl Nampti

'The footprints of the Heart-of-the-Daybreak!
I saw them a long while in the dew
   before the sun swept them away;
the small footprints of Nampti
that make my heart sing.'

K., C.

TOTIUS (J. D. DU TOIT)

FORGIVE AND FORGET

Lest thou forget the things
which thine eyes have seen

A green and growing thorn-tree
stood right against the track
where long spans of oxen
passed to the north and back.

But one day as it grew there
a wagon rode it down,
the big wheels cut a pathway
across the bright green crown.

'Scrub, as I passed, you scratched me,
struck me a sly thorn-thrust;
therefore my great wheels today
have ground you to the dust.'

The wagon rolling onward
was gone behind the hill;
slowly the thorn came upright,
slowly, by its own will.

Its loveliness was shattered,
its young bark broken through;
one place the sapling body
was nearly cut in two.

But slowly, surely upright
the stricken tree has come,
and healed its wounds by dropping
the balm of its own gum.

In course of time the hurt-marks
fade where the wheels had lunged –
only one place endures
that cannot be expunged.

The wounds grew healed and healthy,
with years that come and go,
but that one scar grew greater
and does not cease to grow.

D.

C. LOUIS LEIPOLDT

THE BANDED COBRA

The copper cobra comes out of his slit
   On the ridge and slides around
'The rain has fallen; the veld is wet,
   And wet the red-gold ground.'
The meercat comes, his eyes two gleams,
   And watches bolt-upright.
The ancient porcupine says: 'It seems
   It will rain again tonight.'
But the lizard squeaks: 'Why, that's not rain?
   It's red and sticky and dark:
Such rain will you ever see again –
   So smooth, so fine, so stark?'
And the wise rock-owl weighs in his words:
   'It's blood, it's human blood!
It's living blood at the bushes' roots
   That feeds them in its flood.'

K., C., M.

ON MY OLD RAMKIEKIE

On my little guitar
   With only one string
I play in the moonlight
   Any old thing.

I sing of Adam
   And Eve and the Fall
Of old Paradise –
   'Mad!' they call.

So say the people
  When they hear me play,
Dusk kisses my cheek in its
  Velvet way.

With the moon to listen
  And the nodding stars,
I'm the champion of all who
  Play guitars.

What if they say I'm
  Daft or silly,
If the river reeds listen
  And the lily?

And what of my friends –
  Who think me a loon –
If the stars keep nodding
  And the moon?

On my little guitar,
  One string to it now,
I play in the moonlight
  Any old how.

D.

C. M. VAN DEN HEEVER

THE FALLEN ZULU COMMANDER

Your body gleams like copper on the veld
and grass-ears shed on you
their morning dew,
here where you sleep
your final sleep.
Snow-white your feathers shudder still
as though in battle, but here beside you
a stream of blood has soaked into the sand;
your hand
lies nerveless, slack and grey
beside the flame-sharp assegai.
At Ungungundhlovu your king
will wait for you,
his hand upraised to shade his eyes
that rove out to the furthest blue
where you went fighting.
He will await the thundering feet,
the rattle of the shield,
the oxtails flashing white on dancing legs,
inflaming, fierce and wild.
For you the hilltops call
and by her fire at evening's fall
a lonely Zulu girl will wait,
eyes staring till the break of day.
The sun on fire along the hills
will wake the cow-herds,
their song will echo in the kloofs
against the morning mist,
and all will live and laugh again
though you are gone.

And when the warriors march again,
the hills leap with their frantic dance
the hide shields rattle and the spear-points flash
high in the sun,
then you sleep on
and deep your sleep,
your feathers scattered far by sun and rain,
your body with its under-glow of copper
gone, and you?

Grass-seeds will shed, the cows
and oxen low, and life call out,
but you?
Here where you lay the sheep will browse.

K., C.

N. P. VAN WYK LOUW

THE LITTLE CHISEL

Here in my hands a small cold-chisel,
I tap it and it rings;
and I hone it and I stone it
until its bright edge sings.

I prop a pebble on a rock:
– you've got to get this clear:
a chisel that's a real cold-chisel
can crack a boulder sheer –

I slam it with my chisel edge,
its toughness is a gift:
straight the pebble flies apart
as clean as on a rift:

next, under my ten fingers split,
the granite rock divides,
below my feet I start to feel
the softened earth subside,

and dark the seam runs through my land
and cleaves it to the core –
so a chisel cuts that truly is
a chisel, or what's it for?

Then with two gold-red chasms
the planet falls in two
and down the rockfalls boiling,
drains the ocean flat and blue

and in the day I see the night
below me open far
with a crack that from my chisel blow
runs to the furthest star.

                                        C., K.

BALLAD OF THE DRINKER IN HIS PUB

Meshed in a glow of nickel, glass
and steel, I sit and linger
and see the light gleam through the beer
and through my web-like fingers.

What does it matter if their eyes
pry in upon my silence here?
Or did I scream out unawares
and then forget? – The mirror's clear;

I break the world up through my glass,
make it dissolve; then slowly settle
back to a placid gleam – I know
how shivering frail it is and brittle;

and suddenly my tears well up:
to see how fragile is this earth,
how it is jeered at and betrayed,
no one has pity for its worth . . .

but those who laugh shall never know –
I huddle in the corner here,
trace on my table with a nail
the pentagram with bitter beer.

Now they have all become so grave
and deep in many other things:
and I hang tangled in the mirrors
and stir in eerie planes and rings;

and every terror threatens me
from the unbroken rooms that hem
me round whose silent doors lead out
to what strange nights and alleys, dim

with other moons and other light? . . .
death's level lakes are grey and brack
but this small world of glittering glass
still oscillates, now taut now slack.

All things in which my soul believes,
I'm traitor to, and in me, still
like drip of rain, falls, bead by bead
the arid chaplet of my will.

Now I'm shut within myself and dark;
some tranquil thing stirs round beyond;
a pulse is beating in my eyes
like bubbles rising in a pond.

But of a sudden when some hand
is laid on what I hold most dear,
I slip the knife free from its sheath
furiously to slash and tear.

Why are we not kept safe and sealed
from all the bitter light, the pain and hurt?
why the grey open nerves not closed?
and all the shutters of the heart?

But everything I longed to do
re-lives . . . and God, in my fixed stare
should anyone who sees me now
of what I hide become aware!

Now, even now, I may not say it
but look about me, calm, resigned.
If I can get out through that door,
I'll find perhaps what I desired.

Here I remain now, warm, as if in mud
broiled in a swamp all day.
And frighteningly I start to learn
how all bright things decay.

K., C., M.

THE GODS ARE MIGHTY

The gods are mighty and lonely in the night
and hang like yellow fruit against the tree;
but I stare down in the small shaft
of this sunbeam, and think with no piety:

I know the final great dream of my breed
– my eyes too faint to reach the stars' terrain,
and Meaning, yes, I know is more than Blood –
but blood is manifest, and words are vain.

C.

FROM THE BALLAD OF EVIL

Do you know me now?
Have you looked in the glass,
do you know yourself?

When you'd flee from the burning
city for life,
I'll go along
hand in hand like a wife.

*

Many think they know
my face by sight,
but I'm too lustrous
too close to the light,
and if they wish warning
or wisdom be heard,
I speak as they utter
in each echoing word;

and the swift ones flee,
from whom?   to where?
I am not hideous
nor am I fair,
and where they flee,
they carry me too
in the grey-white grooves
their nerves run through.

Do you know enough?
Do you know whether
whom God made one
belong together?

*

I am your being's
underground,
I walk at your heel
like a faithful hound.

When God in joy
and play let fall
from his hand the earth,
the silver ball,
was I the chaos
it floated in,
the wind, the formless
emptiness?

Though you are radiant
and tall and free
don't believe that you
have done with me,
or my close staying
the course shall fail:
although I'm the dog,
I hold the trail,

on each horizon
I shall bay
and when God's spirit
in the sun's pure ray
shines in lovelier form
than *yours* can be,
then I shall be radiant
and tall and free.

Oh where will you go
and by what ship?
the world is fire
and flint and chip,
and if you would fly
from the city on fire,
I'll go hand in hand
like the one you desire.

Do you know me now?
Have you looked in the glass
that mirrors you?

D.

OH THE INCONSTANT

Oh the inconstant child: young girl
fantasy-making, fantastic, neurotic –
bound forever to the hardest:
wood never could be hard enough for her knife;

lime was too crumbling
(granite again beyond her forbearance),
'form' she had in her, to her – oh the light
play-haunches that filled a universe –

but the role of free hetaira was
concentration-camp wire parting
her from the double bed and babies
and the too wide sheet plus the pillow;

the cool sheet, and the separated pillows
were two mountains and a finlandic mere
between her and her 'sanctity',
between her bestowal and her desire.

K., C.

AT DAWN THE LIGHT WILL COME

At dawn the light will come
and be quiet, and stay
and know he must not wake her up;
and then the day –

he who rises without mercy
out of sleep over good and ill –
will only for her innocence
for one short hour be still

(oh how we fall awake
and in that sorrowing bed
with a small fin try to row
against the watershed, and

back-paddle where the stream
still flows with dream and flash,
into and against the dam-break
a small golden gold fish)

but: then high noon will stand
above her too and scorch her skin,
talk loud and be the world we know
and each word gather in

that she might say in double
sense and loving style;
her little systems in his hand,
held now in his smile;

then he will wait himself awhile
till evening comes mild,
and it will weep about her wish
silent about the child.

K., C.

ARMED VISION

The Visage becomes armed: within:
the small, thin, sheltering soul:
less than Light: other than light: Light:

roundabout: the heavy brain
a kind of ragout, breakfast porridge,
jellyfish; and roundabout:

skull: for the most part lime:
tougher than rocklime, yes, but
maybe something less hard

than lime that is just stone. Then:
skin with daybreak there
and there, and a crack

that is called a 'mouth'
out of which miracles
shower in the subtracted

vulgar fractions which are 'time':
it was all armour – so far –
and ruse: word, mouth, skull,

brain; back, driven back to
the threshold! but then farther: play:
steel visor, mask;

fencing-mask, make-up, smile:
red on the cheek and the lip:
play at hide-and-go-seek:

game that sends rings out still
wider and wider: away
away from the small, sheltering

wronged, indignant
thing which looks down into
the ashpit: and arms itself.

C., K.

UYS KRIGE

THE SOLDIER

In this desolation
of an ashen world
that slowly becomes more fluid,
losing gradually its vague outlines
in a yet more ashen sky,
a single soldier
trudges alone
along the dusty desert track.

And Wajir Fort lies far, lies far
underneath the first pale star.

One soldier
alone
in this immensity
of sand, scrub and stone,
in this limitless dusk
draining the last light,
trudging, trudging out of sight
into the gathering gloom, the Ethiopian night.

And Wajir Fort
– only oasis in this nothingness, this lack
of human life, to which goes wandering each camel track;
where through the thorn-tree leaves at noon at times
    there is the rustle of a breeze,
the throb of heat recedes a step, there comes a
    little coolness and a little ease;
where there are palms that dipping to the moon glint
    with the sheen of shells

and water, sweet clear water, at the bottom of cool
    shafts, deep in the ancient wells:
sole outpost in this waste
where a man may find warm voices, lamplight, wine
    and bread to taste –
lies far, lies far
underneath the first pale star.

He trudges through the dust
a single grey speck
against the greyer grey
of the domed heavens,
the level earth,
this limbo
where the day meets,
mingles with the night.

And Wajir Fort lies far, lies far
underneath the first pale star.

But while the soldier trudges
trudges on
his shadow, slowly, stretches out,
has slid over a broad lava patch, slipped
in among the thorn-trees.

The soldier's shadow
falls over the desert.

The soldier's shadow
falls over Africa.

Rigid and firm, black, stark in its threat
the soldier's shadow falls
wide over the world.

And Wajir Fort lies far, lies far
underneath the first pale star.

K.

SWALLOWS OVER THE CAMP

An unreal silence
rules in the camp.
The afternoon glows
gold as a lamp.

The leaves are falling
winter in the air
and Europe sinks
in shame, despair.

The autumn dies
serene and slow.
The camp stands in
a gentle glow.

The swallows glide
above the gate,
and all the world
is warped with hate.

Marrow and blood
this rot devours.
I give myself
to the quiet hours . . .

But in me twists
a sudden cramp,
loud in my heart
I hear the bombers stamp.

Over all borders
the gunfire swells.
Shall we find peace again?
From what deep wells?

The swallows come,
the swallows soar.
And we, shall we
find love once more?

The bombs strike towns
to dust and litter.
But here the swallows
twitter, twitter . . .

O swallows like
a black brocade
that swing above
the barricade

beyond the wire
in ring on ring
over our heads
you sing and sing

as if sheer in that vault of air
singing without cease
you are the very voice
itself of peace,

and going south
remember me
as at flight's end
beyond the sea

you hover lightly
loop and dive
over the red roof
where Eulalia lives . . .

Then sing for her,
sing with joy too
till she looks up
entranced at you.

And skimming by her
say softly then
I'll come again
yes, I'll come again

and that my dreams
may send her rest.
Give her, swallows,
my tenderness.

K., C.

FARM GATE

Blood-red the aloes flank
the winding road.
As if aflame with leaping sparks
each fire-lily glows.
But nothing, nothing stirs . . . only
a breeze that flows
and seems to pause and waver where
the grass-seed grows.

Above, the blue, blue sky;
and far below, the falling stream
drifts through the orchards with
a flash of green.
And no sound breaks the hovering peace
of this still mountain scene.

Now after all the years I'll open
a gate again.
Where have my paths
till now not led
to bring me to this farm-road gate
with all illusions shed
but hope, hope in my heart
and clear dreams in my head?

The gate stands in
a maroola's shade.
A wholeness in me, harmony
and no bitterness, no hate.
I lift the catch . . . and in my heart
open a gate.

K., C.

DISTANT VIEW

On the bare mountain
a pony and its rider alone.
Caught in that static glow, stockstill,
man, horse: a black statue in stone.

Heights, depths, ravines and peaks
where the rock-silence sings
and in the deep and hidden kloofs
the far murmurings

of torrents leaping free.
The day, yet lonelier, dies in each lonely tree.

The moon butts at the Western rim
with its impala-horn bone-white.
The day's end lingers there . . . each peak a pinnacle
of peace, O world on world of light

so rich and calm! above the hills and valleys,
villages white and still as in a dream:
radiant glow, timeless flood above this wide,
wide world of silence, light, light without edge or seam!

O people of my race, though torn from me,
bound ever to me, heart and spirit and hand,
be great and broad and strong, be free
and full of peace and light as this southern land!

K., C.

ENCOUNTER

Over the black mountain, across the black bay, into the
       black night and beyond
the black wind blows.
And the sea bares its white teeth at the gaunt cliffs
as it snarls and sways, still comes and goes.

Midnight. No star. No light. An empty road flanked by
       the shut rich houses.
And buffeted by the blind
black wind roaring at the sky, the sea, a man
treads the wastes of his own mind.

Darkness and desolation and a sick despair
with no love flowing
gently as water over the hard rock of the heart
– only the black wind blowing

over the creeds and the classes, the continents,
over the seas and the ships
when suddenly beside the road a light leaps from the dark
and the mind slips

back from its far wanderings to this bleak road above
       the cliffs where the spray
is like the beating of cold wings
against the eyes and the gull's thin cry is lost
in the wind's thunderings.

In a paraffin tin a fire leaps, falls, then leaps again
where a black man stands
wrapped in his ragged coat before a half-built house,
warming his hands.

He throws a greeting into the tearing wind.
The cry returns.
And then he smiles: flash of white teeth and broad black
      laugh!
This flame like a comet burns.

O steadfast flame
in the black night,
these wastes are peopled now,
I walk in your light!

K.

D. J. OPPERMAN

FABLE OF THE SPECKLED COW

From hollows of a tree
came cattle herds, and now
my brother chose
for himself the speckled cow.

I pushed him down a cliff,
he fell in a crack,
then a crow came and sat
on the speckled cow's back.

Smear fat on a stone
aim straight, kill the pest,
then a thousand feathers settle
north, south, east, west –

a thousand crows settle
on the blood, on the rock . . .
Oh where shall I hide
from the stipples that peck?

C., K., M.

CHRISTMAS CAROL

Three outas from the bleak Karoo
saw the star, believed the angel true,

took knobsticks and three bundles with
and set forth along a jackal path,

following that bright and moving thing
that shone on shanty, rock and spring,

on zinc and sacking of District Six –
in a broken bottle a candle flicks

where salt fish hangs and donkeys jib,
and lights them kneeling by the crib.

Biltong, sheep fat and eggs they've piled
humbly before God's small brown child,

with hymn and prayer for thanks, they tell
that a child will save *this* folk as well . . .

And on her nest throughout the whole affair
a bantam clucks with a suspicious stare.

D.

WATER WHIRLIGIGS

How long shall you and I be bound
within this sweet enchanted round

of me and you, of me and you?
It rings you round, it rings me too

as we escape with a subtle sense
of shifting aim and violence.

Oh you and I! Oh you and . . . with a start
are terrified apart . . .

Oh where are you? Oh where are you?
It rings me round, it rings you too

with loop enlooped time slips away
tangling us in disarray.

Oh will no ending ever be:
The ring round you, the ring round me

reiteration with no rhyme
through the endless wastes of time?

With patience and impatience round and round
from restlessness will ever rest be found?

What weary years must still be spent
in all this crazed embitterment

of you and me, of you and . . . with a start
are terrified apart . . .

Oh where are you? Oh where are you?
It rings me round, it rings you too,

encircled still both you and I,
the time goes by, the time goes by.

C., K.

FABLE

Under a dung-cake
with the rain in spate
two earthworms held
a terse debate

on 'you' and 'me'
and 'my native land',
on 'my mud-hut
was first to stand'.

A casual spade
by chance sank through,
the earthworms both
were chopped in two:

Four earthworms now
jerk slimily along
the 'I's' and the 'you's'
doubt where they belong.

In the next thick mush
of a meeting place
politely each
greets his own face.

                                                 C.

ELISABETH EYBERS

HAGAR

There is no quenching of the other thirst,
my son, my son. A woman's salt tears roll
corrosively; when as a babe I nursed
you at my breast, they seared your very soul.

Three lives have strangely shaped my destiny:
Abraham, promoting me to pride and shame,
bestowed his brief benignity on me,
fertility my virtue and sole aim.

Then Sara came: how enviable remain
her easy laugh, her guile, her certainty,
to me, who tasted naught but infamy.

You are the third: my loneliness, my pain
have shed their wan submission and of late
been tempered to a man's defiant hate.

(translated by the Author)

RÖNTGEN PHOTOGRAPH

Regard her well – the austere face
with fixed gaze on some distant place
assures you, there are portraits none
more flattering than the skeleton
all virtues clearly to define
and rub out every tender line:
the mouth is never hurt nor shy
and see here the unwavering eye;

the shoulders firm and horizontal
– crossbeam of the druggist's scale –
and all this gleaming frame of bone
within the tissue's twilit zone
exquisite in its shape, design
and, fadeless to the touch of time,
like every valid work of art
reduced to the essential part.

Utterly trivial is the rest,
edgeless and drifting through the mist:
with branching veins the heart hangs there
caught in its shadowy trellised lair;
and channels – entrails, lymph and blood –
sway like seaweed in the flood
and filmy above the pelvic streams
swims that which holds desire and dreams,
unintimate in its nudeness lies
and the sweetness of the sex denies . . .

All grief and ecstasy and pain
were they a phantom of the brain?

C., K., M.

NARRATIVE

A woman grew, with waiting, over-quiet.
The earth along its spiralled path was spun
through many a day and night, now green, now dun;
at times she laughed, and then, at times, she cried.

The years went by. By turns she woke and slept
through the long hours of the night, but every day
she went, as women go, her casual way,
and no one knew what patient tryst she kept.

Hope and despair tread their alternate round
and merge into acceptance, till at length
the years have only quietness in store.

And so at last the narrative has found
in her its happy end: this tranquil strength
is better than the thing she's waiting for.

(translated by the Author)

SLEEP-WALKING CHILD

She never was quite one of us
but this night never was so far.

Now like a goshawk in a snare
the soul that wrestles day by day
in the close cell of bone and blood
takes vengeance on its binding form:
to depths beyond the bounds of sleep
as if a wide and gloomy flood
had swept her there, out of her warm
small bed she rose and slipped away,
and cunning with an art beyond
her waking sense, though unaware,
down the steep spiral of the stair
took flight, unlocked the heavy door
and drifted through the autumn night.

Drifted? But anyone who walks
upright and firm nor lifts a hand
to grope in fear knows where he goes:
does she recall that shoreless land
from which life summoned her
and search for something left behind,
some lost thing we no longer yearn?
Precise and purposeful her steps,

she picks her way wide-eyed but blind
as though across an arching span,
her night-dress thin and fluttering,
past shadows crouching black, to gain
the street soft-footed on sharp stones,
until she wakes, so far from home,
at last to cold and fear and pain.

How will she through our little maze
ever in future thread her ways?

C., K., N.

SNAIL

My softness heaves its spiral canopy:
another roof would be too much to bear.
At home I'm sunk, abroad I'm still at sea,
awkward antennae fumble everywhere.

Hermaphrodite the ruttish ocean spewed
up from the ooze, on dry land I endure
a living thirst by day and night renewed,
and know, except slow death, no certain cure.

(translated by the Author)

OLGA KIRSCH

WORDSPINNING

Little dark Cape girl why is it you roam
through the leaf-stripped winter streets? *Palace, home* . . .

Where in your sleeveless dress with patch and darn
now that the dusk creeps in? *Pigsty, barn* . . .

For I am going home; cold is your path
while indoors wood is crackling on the hearth,

and white and neat the table's ready laid,
my soft bed waiting warm and snugly made.

Then what is it your eyes say, dark and bright?
That God's the God of children who are white?

BLOCKHOUSE

The rock foundation of the fort was dread,
hatred has closed the doors up one by one.
The builder at the loophole grips his gun
And to read the wall-script dares not turn his head.

C.

S. J. PRETORIUS

THE MADMAN

Within the thin
confines of this cell
behind the skin
and the high
windows of the eye
two people dwell:

a madman he,
the other, me.

He with groan and shriek
but I afraid to speak.

Less strongly every hour I fight
against him through the cramped-in night,
and as he wins his screams are hurled
in fury at God and at the world.

In this small boundary
of flesh and bone
are two. Insane
is he,
the other, Me.

K., C.

G. A. WATERMEYER

HARVEST TIME

Twelve years old, my father put
the sickle in my hand:
'You'll bend your back this summer, son,
and sweat into the land.

'I taught you this when you were small,
the duck and then the swing,
knee-thrust and one quick jerk
the firm twist of the string.

'No more I'll lead the mowers' line,
the blood like water in my wrist;
but as you walk the stubble fields
let your hand remember this:

'Here below the Sneeuberg's rim
where Richmond's lands they reap
no man ever cut his swath
ahead of my sickle's sweep . . .'

With brazier and with skin kaross
from far came reapers through the gloom –
Bloukrans, Bethesda, Graaff-Reinet
and Katberg's green wild broom.

And there the cock of Spandouskop
yellow and tall leads all the rest,
with windmill arms bolts through the corn
like a rank wind from the west.

At break of day the corn-stalks bend,
shake cool dew on the ground;
at sun-up sweetly the sickles sing
with a long rasping sound.

Twelve noon, and we seek the shade –
like a two-year ox gone in the knees
after its first long highroad trek
I hit the cool of poplar trees.

Two o'clock the heavens and
the earth are one white flood,
and every clod an ash-blue coal,
the corn as red as blood.

At five my eyes roll wildly
as a foal about to drop;
but casual humming by my side
skips the bull of Spandouskop.

'Go it, Basie! Give it stick!
Here we ride with the snaffle hard;
must you stare forever at
the bell-iron in the yard?'

O God! And will this sluggish sun
never drop down to the hill,
and will this wind with tongue of flame
never have scorched its fill . . .?

At eight the wheat-sheaf crackles
under my dizzy head,
but through my brain and joints the sun
and sickles dance their tread.

From red at dawn to twilit dusk
the sickles flicker on the land;
my back is tanned and tough with pain,
I snatch with a nimbler hand.

Old year's Eve – and by tonight
we'll mow the last wide swath
when the moon comes over Kompasberg
white-sailed and rides her path.

It's the stallion of Spandouskop
and I who tear through the yellow grain
and take the hissing sickle-song
way out in front again.

Duck and gather, duck and gather,
bend down the ears and reap.
Three snatches make a handful,
six handfuls to a sheaf.

Here's Sneeuberg valley's tow-head lad
who glides like a rinkhals snake
and to the far end of the land
cuts wide his glistening wake.

'Swing wide, old Tatta, wider!
Why run your mouse-path with these snips?
Here every man must cut his line –
don't say you've had your chips?'

It's Sneeuberg valley's young Boer this,
at the spearhead calls no stop,
and every sickle-arm's left far,
far back to graze the crop.

B., K., C.

SHEILA CUSSONS

1945

Europe lies in ruins: a black headline story,
staccato, blunt; a teacup prattle.
Europe is a crater in the firmament, no more.

But through the crossword puzzle of rigid steel
the rain-grey pigeons tumble, flap and soar
longing for broods, to nest and mate again
above the black cathedral's tortured shell.
An Archangel lies in the rain's wet gleam, and rust devours
quietly his silver wing, the cosmos of his silver brain.

C., K.

BAREND TOERIEN

CAMPI FLEGREI

This landscape demands: open vowels,
umbrella pines, the cypresses' oval
phalli. Washed by the mare nostrum
stand the rounded columns.

Not here the blond flickering of beech or birch,
the elm or lime or other northerners;
not here their Gothic superfluousnesses
or the diphthongs of their wild landscapes.

The dark pines, rounded by the sun
flame up shimmering from the ground.
Above, the goatherd blows his flute
and calls the cattle up the slope.

(translated by the Author)

QUATRAIN

My bloodstream chokes on gall and spleen;
that's why I wake up slowly and with a groan.
How does one get acclimatized
to the day-long bitter taste which is one's own?

(translated by the Author)

THE FIRMAMENT DISPLAYS ON HIGH

The firmament displays on high
vast clouds of nebulae from where
my rough forefathers Isengrim
from separate constellations stare

and frown on me from far above.
I hurt them daily, probably.
My aim's to show them that I love
them (they are in the majority).

I therefore grant them a slight nod
though they withhold favour and smile
and go my way, sleeping calm,
and happy to be alive meanwhile.

(translated by the Author)

YOUTH

Before daybreak, before dew breaks,
the crystal cobwebs fall and crumble,
the stallion the red stallion whinnies in the stable
when I drop the catch of the door handle.

A cock-crow suddenly tears the net
of mist in which the pines are caught
and the stallion the red stallion, oh the excitable
stamps on the steaming floor of the stable.

The men with their fireflies are at the kraal
– behind glass? – under water?
then the stallion bursts out of the stable
letting fly a rain of sand and gravel.

That afternoon with blue – and oh yes, there were
mirages islanding the field –
the stallion neighed atop of a mare. Oh noble
Ulysses! Oh Zeus! before the tumble.

(translated by the Author)

ABSENT DAUGHTER

In the fall-out of daisies on the rockland
in the copper or yellow rockgrain and whorls of Table
                    Mountain,
its moss and lichen iguana engravings
in bark chips and leaves and overlapping planes in rock pools
your toys left their traces, you muddle head.

I'm back in my room, staring, surprised at my hand full
                    of shells
that twist in my palm, trying to get free.
Throw them away and don't look where they fall!
Wentletrap, wentletrap, whelk –

Ah, there's that chanting again!

Don't lock me out, wentletrap
Don't lock me out, staircase,
stalk bearing the rich calyx, her room
of furry animals with eyes of daisies and lichen and
                    klipfish
staring at me from her sleeping arms.

                              (translated by the Author)

INGRID JONKER

―

PREGNANT WOMAN

I lie under the crust of the night singing,
curled up in the sewer, singing,
and my bloodchild lies in the water.

I play that I'm a child:
gooseberries, gooseberries and heather,
kukumakrankas* and anise,
and the tadpole glides
in the slime in the stream,
in my body
my foam-white image
but sewer O sewer,
my bloodchild lies in the water.

Still singing fleshrose our bloodsong,
I and my yesterday,
my yesterday hangs under my heart,
my marigold, my cradling world,
and my heart that sings like a cicada,
my cicada-heart sings like a cicada;
but sewer O sewer,
my bloodchild lies in the water.

*Kukumakrankas – Hottentot word for a starlike Cape flower.

I play that I'm happy:
look where the firefly sparkles!
the moon-disc, a wet snout that quivers –
but with the morning, the limping midwife,
grey and shivering on the sliding hills,
I push you out through the crust into daylight,
O sorrowing owl, great owl of the daylight,
free from my womb but besmeared,
with my tears all smeared
and tainted with despair.

Sewer O sewer
I lie trembling, singing,
how else but trembling
with my bloodchild under your water . . .?

C., K.

THE CHILD WHO WAS SHOT DEAD
BY SOLDIERS AT NYANGA

The child is not dead
the child lifts his fists against his mother
who shouts Afrika! shouts the breath
of freedom and the veld
in the locations of the cordoned heart

The child lifts his fists against his father
in the march of the generations
who are shouting Afrika! shout the breath
of righteousness and blood
in the streets of his embattled pride

The child is not dead
not at Langa nor at Nyanga
nor at Orlando nor at Sharpeville
nor at the police post in Philippi
where he lies with a bullet through his brain

The child is the dark shadow of the soldiers
on guard with their rifles, saracens and batons
the child is present at all assemblies and law-giving
the child peers through the windows of houses and into the
    hearts of mothers
this child who wanted only to play in the sun at Nyanga is
    everywhere
the child grown to a man treks on through all Africa
the child grown into a giant journeys over the whole world

Without a pass

C., K.

25 DECEMBER 1960

(For Dylan Thomas)

Ward 130 in the passage on the right.
It's five in the morning and the milk-cart
has gone by with its horses, their eyes gleaming
in the bayonet-points of the street lights.
25 December 1960.
The children sleep
in Christmas stockings between satellites
hobby-horses, revolvers and toffees.
Sleep before the sirens of the sun
before the bombers of the butterflies.
Sleep in your Christmas stockings and candles.
On Hospital Hill stands a blazing tree.
Ward 130 in the passage on the right.
'Sure he drank a bottle of brandy
and lay for hours in an oxygen tent.
You know he was an alcoholic from
his first glass.' (Look, the day's
bright gun-barrel takes aim over the city!)
'Ah yes but, he himself once said
he had a harking after his dead God.

His final words? No
he lay quiet and with eyes wide open.'
Ward 130. He's been attended to
the eyes closed the hands already folded,
the whole room like a shield uplifted.

And on the windowsill and against the light
the praying mantis in unending prayer.

C., K.

BEGIN SUMMER

(*For Simone*)

Begin summer and the sea
a cracked-open quince
the sky like a child's
balloon
far above the water
Under the umbrellas
like stripy sugarsticks
ants of people
and the gay laugh of the bay
has teeth of gold

Child with the yellow bucket
and the forgotten pigtail
your mouth surely is a little bell
tiny tongue for a clapper
You play the sun all day
like a ukulele

C., K.

I DON'T WANT ANY MORE VISITORS

I don't want any more visitors
not with cups of tea espresso and especially not brandy
I don't want to hear them waiting on winged letters
I don't want to hear them lying awake in their eyeballs
    while
the other sleeps wide like the horizon over his eyebrows
and what do I want to know about their same old ailments
the one without ovaries and the other with leukaemia
the child without a music-box and the old man
who's now forgotten that he's deaf
the caprice of death in the robots of green
the people living by the sea as though in the Sahara
the betrayers of life with the face of death and of God

I want to be myself travelling with my loneliness
like a walking-stick
and believe I'm still unique

                  (translated by the Author)

LOST CITY

In the rain that has passed by
faraway day and lost city
of acorns and doves full of daybreak

my hands were the one small squirrel
quick to be shy but prepared
faraway day and lost city

through all the people you have come
with a simple smile
as if from a long journey

238

and the rain that has passed by
has warmed itself against my body
the rain of smoke and ochre

that smells of your clean-washed hands
of warm doves and the open
orange poppy of the sky

C., M.

THE FACE OF LOVE

Your face is the face of all the others
before you and after you and your eyes calm as a blue
dawn breaking time on time
herdsman of the clouds
sentinel of the white iridescent beauty
the landscape of your confessed mouth that I have explored
keeps the secret of a smile
like small white villages beyond the mountains
and your heartbeats the measure of their ecstasy

There is no question of beginning
there is no question of possession
there is no question of death
face of my beloved
the face of love

C.

I DRIFT IN THE WIND

Free I have my own self-reliance
from graves and from deceptive friends
the hearth which I have cherished glares at me now
my parents have broken themselves off from my death
the worms stir against my mother my father
clasps his groping hand limp against the sky
free I believe my old friend has forsaken me
free I believe you have toppled the mountains in me
free my landscape smells of bitter sun and blood

What will become of me
the cornerstones of my heart bring no fulfilment
and my landscape is hardened in me
brooding and bitter but open

My nation
follow my lonely fingers
people be warm-hearted in yourselves
veiled in the sun of the coming days

My black Africa
follow my lonely fingers
follow my absent image
lonely as an owl
and the forsaken fingers of the world
alone like my sister
My people have rotted away from me
what will become of the rotten nation
a hand cannot pray alone.

The sun will cover us
the sun in our eyes forever covered
with black crows

C.

ADAM SMALL

THERE'S SOMETHIN'

You can stop me
drinking a pepsi-cola
at the cafe
in the Avenue
or goin' to
an Alhambra revue,
you can stop me doin'
some silly thing like that
but o
there's somethin' you can
never never do;
you can stop me
boarding a carriage
on the Bellville run
white class
or sittin' in front
of the X-line
on the Hout Bay bus,
you can stop me doin'
some silly thing like that
but o
there's somethin' you can
never never do;
you can stop me
goin' to Groote Schuur
in the same ambulance
as you

or tryin' to go to Heaven
from a Groote Kerk pew
you can stop me doin'
some silly thing like that
but o
there's somethin' you can
never never do;
true's God
you can stop me doin'
all silly things of that sort
and to think of it
if it comes to that
you can even stop me hatin'
but o
there's somethin' you can
never never do –
you can't
ever
ever
ever stop me
loving
even you!

AFRICAN SECTION

TRADITIONAL

PRAYER TO THE YOUNG MOON

said by X-nanni

Small moon
Hai! young moon
    hai hai!
Young moon speak to me
    hai hai!
    young moon
Tell me of something
    hai hai!
When the sun rises
    you must speak to me
    that I may eat something
you must speak to me about a little thing
    that I may eat
    hai hai!
    Young moon

Recited by the Bushman X-nanni to W. H. I. Bleek in 1855 and
recorded and interpreted by him. This translation, reworked from
Bleek's version, follows the original Bushman pattern. c.

PRAYER TO THE HUNTING STAR, CANOPUS

said by X-nanni

Xkoagu, give me your heart
that you sit with in plenty.
Take my heart, my heart
small and famished without hope
so that like you I too may be full
  for I hunger.

You seem to me full-bellied, Xkoagu
and in my eyes not small
  but I am hungry.

Star, give to me your belly
that fills you with a good feeling,
and you shall take my stomach from me
so you as well can know its hunger.
Give me your right arm too
and you shall take my arm from me,
my arm that does not kill
  for I miss my aim.

Xkoagu, blind with your light
  the Springbok's eyes,
and you shall give me your arm
for my arm that hangs here
that makes me miss my mark.
c. after W. H. I. Bleek

STAR SONG OF THE BUSHMAN WOMEN

related by Dai-Kwain

Does the lily flower open?
The daisy is the flower that opens.
And do you open?
The daisy is the flower that opens.

Song sung by the star Gauun, and especially by Bushman women;
related by Dai-Kwain to W. H. I. Bleek.

THE WIND AND THE BIRD

(*Naron Bushman Song*)

The Wind is a man and goes out from his hut.
As a bird, Xgauwa goes with the Wind:
one with two names are they, Xgauwa and Hise.
The Wind has the bird with him and he walks a little way
but no more: from the earth he rises,
into the sky he shoots up, he soars
and he takes the grass and whirls it far
scatters it so it falls a great distance.
The magician sees the one walking with the Wind,
it is Xgauwa, and the bird speaks to him saying
'I am he who arouses the Wind.'

after W. H. I. Bleek

RE-BIRTH

A prayer to the New Moon related by Dai-Kwain

Young moon, take my face up yonder,
give back to me your face up there,
    take away this pain.

Give me your face, small moon,
that dies, and when you die
living, you return again.
When we see you, and no more we see you
you lie down to sleep and come again.
Give me that I shall be like you
this joy that you possess forever
yonder with you, that living you come back
when we did not see you there.

Once when your child the hare
cried to you, his mother, not to let him die
you told us too that when we died
    we should return again.

c. after W. H. I. Bleek

THE BROKEN STRING

Lament sung by Xaa-ttin for the death of his friend the
magician and rain-maker Nuin-kui-ten; related by Xaa-
ttin's son Dai-Kwain.

They were the people, those who
broke the string for me
    and so
this place was a grief to me
    for what they did.

Since it was that bow-string which broke for me
and its sound no more in the sky, ringing,
hereabouts it feels to me no longer
like it once felt to me
just for that thing.
    For
everything feels as if it stood open before me
empty, and I hear no sound
for they have broken the bow's string for me
and the old places are not sweet any more
    for what they did.

Nuin-kui-ten the magician and rain-maker died from a shot he had
received when going about by night in the form of a lion. Xaa-ttin
laments that the 'former ringing sound in the sky' is no longer
heard by him as it had been in the magician's lifetime, now that
the 'string is broken'.

from W. H. I. Bleek

THE SONG OF NU-NUMMA-KWITEN

Song recited by Hau-kasso about 'White-Mouth', big eater
of meat and swallower of ostrich eggs

Nu-numma-kwiten formerly sang

Hn-n, hn
I kill children who cry
hn-n, hn
I kill children who cry
hn-n, hn
I kill children who cry

A beast of prey Nu-numma-kwiten is
my grandfather used to say that
Nu-numma-kwiten formerly sang

Hn-n, hn
I kill children who cry
hn-n, hn
I kill children who cry

When my grandfather said
we must leave off making a noise
and we called out as we played
he told us Nu-numma-kwiten
in old times came and sang

Hn-n, hn
I kill children who cry
hn-n, hn
I kill children who cry

And when he hears a little child crying there
he follows the sound to it
while the little child is crying there
he, following the sound, goes to it
approaches it stealthily
approaching stealthily
reaches the hut where the child cries.
He springs
springs into the hut.
He catches hold of the little child
he springs, and takes it away.
He goes to swallow it down.
He steals away.

SONG OF THE SPRINGBOK DOES

The springbok doe mothers sang
soothing their children
    A-á hn
    Wai! springbok baby
     sleep for me
    Wai! springbok child
     sleep for me.

after W. H. I. Bleek

SONG OF THE THUNDER

Son of the Thundercloud
the brave loud-speaking Xgoro,
Ah talk softly, talk softly
for I have no guilt.
Bear with me in your pity
for I am weak and stand stunned.
You, O Xgoro
son of the Thundercloud.

> Recorded in 1860 by Theophilus Hahn, the
> language being now virtually extinct

DANCE-SONG OF THE LIGHTNING

Chorus of villagers

Hai! daughter of the Thundercloud
daughter-in-law of the spirit Fire,
you are she who has killed my brother
and so gone without sorrow
and lain down in your lair.

Solo, the Lightning

Yes true, it was I took your brother
and I killed him with joy.

Chorus

So now you lie in the hole, your lair:
you have painted your body with red ochre
shining red like the body of Xgoro.
Daughter-in-law of the Fire, you do not
as others, flow at the menses –
you wife of the Copper-bodied man.

> From T. Hahn

HOW DEATH CAME

The Moon, they say, called Mantis,
sent him with life to people saying:
Go to men and tell them this –
   As I die and dying live,
   you too shall die and dying live.
Mantis started, took the word.
Then Hare stopped him by the path,
he said: What, insect, is your errand:
Mantis answered: I am sent by Moon,
by that one, I must say to men –
   As he dies and dying lives
   they too shall die and dying live.
Hare the quick-tongue said to him:
Why run? You are shaky on your legs.
Let me go, I outrun the wind.
Hare ran, he came to men and said:
Moon sent me with this word –
   As I die and dying perish
   you shall die and utterly die.
Hare raced again to Moon,
told him all that he had said to men.
The Moon said dark with anger:
How is it you dared tell them
this thing I never said?
He took up wood, a sharp fire-log,
with one blow in the face
struck down the Hare. He split
the lying Hare's lip to this day.

From the MSS of Hottentot folklore in the
original language in the Grey Collection,
Cape Town, quoted by W. H. I. Bleek in
Hottentot Fables and Tales, 1864

HUNTER'S PRAYER

O Heitsi-Eibib
hai! our forefather,
send luck to me
give into my hand the wild game
let me find honey-comb and sweet roots
and I will sing you my praise.
Are you not our father's father
you, Heitsi-Eibib?

From T. Hahn

HYMN TO TSUI-XGOA

You, O Tsui-Xgoa
you, all-father
you, our father!
Let stream to earth the thundercloud,
give that our flocks may live,
give life to us.
I am so stricken with weakness
I thirst and I hunger.
Allow that I gather and eat the field fruits,
for are you not our first one
the father of fathers,
you, Tsui-Xgoa –
that we may sing to you in praise
that we may measure to you in return,
you, all-father
you, our maker
you, O Tsui-Xgoa.

From Theophilus Hahn, who describes
Tsui-Xgoa as the Supreme Being of the
Khoi-Khoi, as the Hottentots called themselves

ANIMAL SONGS

Hyena

You who make your escape from the tumult,
wide gloomy tree
snatching your share of the kill and bitter the cost;
you walk like a cow gone in the hocks
with your big bumble knees
and the nape of your neck a shag of hair,
your neck all bulging and swollen.
You, devourer of the Namaqua people,
Big-toothed one.

Hyena's song to her Children

The fire threatens
the sling-stone menaces me
the assegais threaten
the gun points death at me,
yet you howl around me for food
my children!
Do I get anything so easily?

Springbok

O sorrow! He is one who jumps
where his mother fears to allow him!
And he bounds down the rocks
rolling himself together like a blanket.

Giraffe

You who descend river by river
over the land, a fire-burnt bush,
you blue one
who looms like a far-off thorn-hill
full of people sitting together.

Baboon

Heretse!
Heretse!
Thin-armed one with the thin hands
and smooth as a bullrush mat,
you walk along with arched neck.
Made light to be lifted up,
you swing yourself up into a tree.
Heretse, you will not die behind that hill
but race your pursuers beyond –
hill over that far-off hill.

Baboon 2

You hollow-cheeked son
of one with such hollow cheeks,
my fellow with the cheek-pouches,
and slung on the high hip-bones,
the big bones of your bottom
with which you sit on the rock edge
and your face too looks like a ridge of stone.

Zebra Stallion

Target of the hunting shepherd boys
whose head is too swift for the throwing-stick –
You dappled fly,
you of the shadow and light
keeping a sharp watch
for those who watch for you!
O you who like a woman
are so full of jealousy.

Zebra

You X-ari bush,
strong-smelling, who rolls in the soft ground
and rises up blanketed by dust.
Split throwing-stick of the shepherd boys,
knob of the hunting stick,
you drive away with your whinnying
the buck stalked by the hunter
and flying, you cross all rivers
as if they were only one.

Lion

Alas! you son of her who is short-eared,
you, the short-eared child,
son of her who tears the kill
you devourer of hot flesh,
son of her whose nose is red from the prey
you with the bloodstained nostrils,
son of her who drinks pit-water,
you, drinker at the water-hole.

Elephant

Tall-topped acacia, you, full of branches,
Ebony-tree with the big spreading leaves.

From *Hottentot Fables and Tales*,
quoted by W. H. I. Bleek

TRADITIONAL

SONG OF THE UNLOVED

I could have wept and howled
Seeing the bridal cattle pass;
Not for me, but for the beautiful ones,
For Thathalasi and suchlike,
Lovely with a high-bridged nose.

C., Ku.

(Recorded by Azariele Sekese)

FUNERAL SONG

Chorus of Women
Now we are left out,
Alone we sit and cry,
Left only to our sorrow
Empty and dull with pain,
And our hearts bruised sore.

A Woman
Ah let God make me a place in the sky
And keep me a cooking pot and a fire.
As I am, I would travel up there –
If I could grow wings like a bird
And fly to him there.

The Widow
Dull and faint is my heart.
When the first dark brings the night
I go out under the eaves,

257

Alone I stand there and listen,
I am quiet and try to hear:
I say to myself he is coming.

Ku., C.

LAMENT FOR A WARRIOR

Sister of the Dead

Women, if we held the oxhide shield
and I had stood by him in battle
he would have come, my mother's son,
he would not have died, our child,
but walking home have said: I fell
only when I tripped up on a stone.

Chorus of women

Ao! has he gone has he gone
and left us here alone?
Tell us, has his soul been sent
never to see us again,
and all of them, all gone
where there's no returning?
Will the earth's womb not be filled,
will the grave have never done!

Ku., C.

Z. D. MANGOAELA

BOAST OF MASOPHA

Masopha, also called Nkau, comes to the place of his over-lord, the King Moshesh, to ask for permission to wage war on the Thembus. The King refuses but offers him compensation – 'the oxen of peace' – which he defiantly slaughters as food for his expedition. He attacks the Thembus on the pretext of avenging his uncle and carries off their cattle.

'I am he who bursts the guarded gate
blocked by the little Bushmen of Chere!
Many fighting-men climbed up seeking like women
this side and that for the easier way,
clambering, panting to be shoved forward.'

Yesterday Nkau stood before Moshesh at the King's place,
to the stronghold he had come to ask for war
but they sent him instead the oxen of peace
fit for cowards, and he spurned them –
he slaughtered them for meat along the way.
Then in the shaded valleys he sat down
and saw the trail led to Letsika.
He sent a spy among the Thembu cattle
who prowled unnoticed by the watching boys.

As the fire caught with red flame-tongues
Nkau, fiery-blooded, who eats the meat hot,
the swooping eagle, son of my lord,
like a hunting-dog he came, fire in his eyes
and fangs bared.

Then he spoke to the fighters of Lioli,
he said: Strike the youths with your assegais,
stab them, throw them as carrion
to the vultures of Ngoniland, jubilant,
the black ones perched among the trees.
O black fury called Letsitsa, brother of Mpinane,
fight and avenge your uncle's murdered head,
blood for the head of Makhabane.

'See then, you men of Kwena,
how I struck back for Makhabane,
I killed even the Thembu king.'

N. M. KHAKETLA

THE WHITE AND THE BLACK

While I'm gone, white mother, kill the fattened oxen
And feed your dear ones well, prime meat and curds
Overspilling so the dogs too lap the juice,
And still enough is left to throw a surplus
To your close kin across the seas.

And you, black mother, hold on firm –
There is a mystery in things to come
And a fierce look lights behind your eyes.
As the world-ball turns around and round
The fleeing partridge finds the forbidden grain.

Ku., C.

B. MAKALO KHAKETLA

LESOTHO

On the navel of the Boer's domain –
that Father of Lambs – and of the Rooinek's place
stands an antheap, an eye-catching target,
a goad to the white one slackened in plenty
where he sits like a king down in the plains
and has his thin-tailed sheep sheared.

These are no termites but the black ants of Mokgatjhane
streaming out by day and by night.
O you fatal paths that run into the Free State,
into the Cape Colony and yonder to Natal,
let devil-thorns and nettles block you
to keep back the Black Ants inside Lesotho!

The strong and youthful girl who loved Moshesh
now is a temptation in the heart of the Boer.
Her ample gall-bladder is the mountain Phofung
and with the splashing of the bile over her body
she Motshwanyane, was lovely beyond praise
and war came, and the bulls kicking up dust.

There are wild dogs in Lesotho,
wild dogs that gnaw bones between their forepaws –
I speak of Makwa and such as he, warriors of Moshesh.
They drew up at Maseru a strong garrison at the gates,
they lay there jealously to watch over the valley
of Moshesh – he, Letlama, son of Mokgatjhane.

Do you imagine, Moselekatse, mere Zulu that you are,
that you could wrestle against Motshwanyane?
She is a youthful girl and strong, all love her,
a skimmer waterbeetle, her body red with ochre –
And you know that she turned down in scorn
the wooing of the handsome Wepener and his like,
yet you dare try your hand! Just who are you?

Motshwanyane is already the bride of Moshesh,
Grandmother Victoria it was fixed the lobola,
the leading cow coming at the full moon in February
and the match made when the March moon was young
and ten oxen were slaughtered for the groom
and they gave two cows as well, a large and a small.

Grandmother Victoria spoke from afar,
she spoke in a voice loud with anger:
'Be no longer obstinate, you Boers;
do not say she was your wife and an adulteress.
Lesotho, the Black Girl, long since was married,
she was taken as his wife by Moshesh.

'Today I speak with no fumbling words:
Call back your stragglers from Lesotho,
call back your unceasing raids;
stifle what grievances you have
for this land lies under Moshesh, he took it;
One bull only in Lesotho – Moshesh.'

He is a tamer who breaks in the untamed;
he made the due rites at the ancestral grave.
Riding, he has firm grip with his legs
and he rode the young heifer with a tight hold
and broke it in and tamed it to his use
so that today they ride it and they need no thong.

Astonishing he is in his wise ways!
He brought with him the three medicine horns
to cure the indolence of his bride.
Above her heart he cut her with his blade
and in the wound rubbed white charms and black;
her eyes gleamed instantly and she began to see!

How fertile is she still, Setshwana, Black woman!
Strong men-children has she borne Moshesh!
The young men wear their black shields on their heads
and on their shoulders fall the hoods of learning,
and round their necks such things unknown of old,
walking with pride and everywhere supreme.

Hybrid cow with the heavy udder,
nations may despise you and in scorn
say you are no hybrid but a weakling beast,
but we who own you ever will sing your praise:
Our first love, you who fill our calabashes up with milk,
often we milk you and you brim our pail.

Ku., C

E. A. S. LESORO

THE MUSCOVY DRAKE

Handsome one, white-black checkered son of the water,
No side-creeping crab, he's a skimmer beetle!
Eyes set with brass like a man in fighting fettle,
And his fine feathers smoothed with butter.

His sandals the skin off an ox's brow,
We know not how warm his paddling claw –
We, mere men who wrap ourselves round
With the sun, the blanket of the poor.

The big fellow, dignified, bowing,
Whispers soft and his secrets go unheard!
And we praise him for his secrecy, knowing
No home is broken by an unsaid word!

Ku., C.

D. G. T. BERENG

THE BIRTH OF MOSHESH

What began that bustle in the village,
Why all the stirring in the yards?
What moves the restless women from hut to hut
Or has the young men glancing round?
What sets menfolk at each other's ears,
Of what dread things do the drums speak;
What starts the hollow bull-horns booming,
Strums on the sounding calabash strings
And what reed notes these on the shrill pipes?
See now the smiling women's faces,
All the young men amazed,
And the elders speaking in tough riddles.

Bright and clear the veld,
Echoes ringing in the hills,
And the sound hung above the peaks
And all the cliff caves rebounding.
The wild beasts roamed uneasily
And the antelopes went skipping away;
The animals went unheeded in this daze of news
And men and women left wondering:

To Libenyane a man-child is born.
He emerged with a shield gripped in his hand.
In his face the people read great deeds
Heralded before they came to be;
And things were dark to ponder.
For men saw plants grow as they watched
And flowers bloom luxuriant,
Stars streamed in the day sky
Like midnight lightnings.

They saw flame-tongues in the sun
And in their huts men laid aside their blankets.
The moon stood still against the sky
Like a shy bride before her husband's father.
Through a cranny the whispering was heard,
The cattle also seemed to listen
And soon their lowing was loud;
The wet-nosed household gods bellowing out,
Lions roaring in the plains
Roar and give way before the King.
Leopards roaring in the krantzes
Roar and give way before the King.
The wild beasts made the world tremble
For him, Moshesh, though but an infant,
Man-child suckled on the milk of antelopes.

Thus and thus we knew Thesele was born
For when born, he Letlama, son of Mokhachane,
When he was born the tribes were glad.
The day the great Lepoqo saw the light
We sang new songs unknown to us
And for us the young girls swung in dance.
Then it was we could say:
Halala! You Zulus of Natal!
We too have a true chief today.
And you on Caledon's banks, see our pride!
We too raise battle shields today;
We stand free at the rock fastness, Thaba Bosio,
Stronghold given by God to Thesele.

Ku., C.

S. D. R. SUTU

NIGHT

Night, and on all sides only the folding quiet,
In the sky the wide staring eyes of the stars:
Looking from them maybe the earth shines too
As winking softly, they watch in their delight
This loveliness that lies asleep in all its peace.

And everywhere around, and coming in on me
Is a great stillness, unutterable silence in the open,
And not a grass-blade nor a single reed that trembles,
No sound rises anywhere, no murmur, nothing;
Night, and on all sides only the folding quiet.

A stirring of the air, a little thing, brushes my cheek,
A faint wind, spirit of life in this night.
The flowers, the wild creatures, all things made on earth
Now are blanketed in quietness and still
As if their hearts were giving thanks to their Creator.

Were I not apart in my own loneliness here
I would say: 'My brother, turn around and look
Far off towards the east along the mountains, gaze
Above the eastern peaks, ours for a little while,
And see what fills my eyes – the golden light!'

And I would say: 'Let us gaze there with new eyes
And side by side as one look at the glory in the sky
The scattering up of gold from the horizon,
A glow that brightens through the far-distant blue
And is touched by rays of white – gaze out there.'

I would say: 'Brother, stand here by my side tonight,
Share this with me, this earth, this sky.'
The moon, gold-skinned ruler of the night, shows her rim –
First a narrow husk, and then – the great round gourd!
And I long to say: 'What lovelier than this!'

You would feel then as I feel, my brother,
Like small children struck by some thing of wonder,
Their faces rapt with smiles and eyes alight
Their small breasts rise and fall, hearts beat –
Then you and I would stamp our feet in joy.

Yet here as I stand single in my loneliness
I cannot shout against the silence of the night.
No sign or sound comes of the laughing-dove
And the owl, familiar of witches, still keeps dumb.
Night, and on all sides only the folding quiet.

The scene moves, now let me turn back to my house,
Shut out the night, eyes closed and roll myself in sleep.
While my heart still brims full with this joy,
Asleep, let dreams untroubled visit me
To wake again and smile and raise up a song.

Night, and on all sides only the folding quiet,
In the sky the wide staring eyes of the stars:
Looking from them maybe the earth shines too.
My star, never hide from me but show my way
That I too may let my light shine through the dark.

Ku., C.

THABA BOSIO

I raced west away from the dawn
and saw the swift darkness flying.
The moon as I looked upwards
shed tears in pity for me
and behind me was the Morning Star.
Urged on with desire and like
a hunter in pursuit I crossed the rim
and the low-topped mountains rose up there,
spaced far, alone, and each peak
smiled to greet the newborn sun.
I asked a woman in her yard the way
to Thaba Bosio; she showed the hill,
showed me a miserable crest beside
the taller peaks – Thaba Bosio, the stronghold.
And unbelieving I made my way towards it –
the sun struck my brow and the sweat rolled.

Mine was like a child's joy running to meet
his mother and the space growing less between them.
An aircraft thundered in the sky, and some space
away I saw a fin-tailed car . . .
these faded and their uproar died,
my heart was filled with long-forgotten things:
Moshesh, warrior among warriors,
with assegai and shield at Thaba Bosio
fighting well, axe and club, stabbing, cracking.
And I heard again his just vaunt:
'It is I, Moshesh, ravager of Kadi, the razor,
shaver of Ramonaheng's beard.'
Wondering, I gazed upwards
searching for the unseen pass –
and no longer heard the droning 'plane
but in my heart the names Moshesh . . . Thaba Bosio.

I saw him come and walk around Bosio,
the muscles strong and living in his limbs,
his sharp darting eye and mind alert,
quick to listen and with firm-set strides.
He, servant of the youths who served their land,
saw at last and scaled the pass, and built a town
and taught them to fight like men.

There at the square, cross-shaped Thaba Bosio
I too saw and climbed the narrow pass:
the ruins told me of the great Moshesh,
they told me of the long-gone Sotho life –
high massive walls of well-cut stone,
the many rooms, the courtyard
ringed around with ancient aloes;
and suddenly my thoughts were with the dead,
I prayed for light to guide my soul.

I saw Moshesh with folded arms sit with his chiefs
and watch the airplanes cross his land
and cars speed on the roads;
he watched his young men leave the borders
to find a living, scatter far and wide,
digging like moles for gold and heaving trucks.
Bitter drink they brew to heat the blood,
and brothers, lacking faith, join bloody fights,
lost to the power of their parents' word.
Sadly Moshesh watched with his warriors;
unsmiling, for they had taught their sons
the chess game they themselves had played
with skill against the whiteman, Wepener;
against Moselekatse, Matowane and Sekonyela.
But their children have not learned –
I saw him and his men look sadly on.
I saw him then bowed in old age
weak in his legs and his blood flowing slow,

the power failing in his mind, ear, eye,
until he turned his thoughts to the Creator
and at God's feet he fell, and sought shelter of the Queen.

At last I saw the grave where he lies sleeping
beside his warriors, and humbly I approached.
I asked myself, could it be ever
that we build Bosio on their ashes
or a fresh shoot sprout finely from this stump?
I knelt down near the resting place of warriors
and seemed to hear a voice:
'Be patient, child of heaven, the time will come.'

Ku., C.

M. A. MOKHOMO

WHEN HE SPOKE TO ME OF LOVE

The day he first spoke to me of love
The day he taught me in those words,
The marvel in my breast, and dreams,
I dreamed even in the middle of the day.
My voice was burnt away, a fire
In my throat licked at my words –
In my pride I stood there quite dumb,
All my face wet with happy tears.
Fear struck fast and heavy at my side
That he might change, and barking dogs
Drive off the bridal cattle brought for me.
I came trembling to him on my knees
As if stooped down in a prayer of love.
My beloved, his voice more sweet,
His young mouth poured a stream of gold.
My great one, he looked long into my face
And my tongue, unstrung, confessed to him.

Ku., C.

DEMETRIUS SEGOOA

PRAISES OF THE TRAIN

I am the black centipede, the rusher with a black nose,
drinker of water at the fountain itself of witches,
and whose spells do you say can bewitch me?
I vanquished the sun, man-eater, and the jet-black dark
where the beasts of prey drink blood by day and night –
I, the centipede, great roarer with an inward roar.

My people named me Traveller-to-the-South.
I have altered, not any more a bearer of burdens,
the black calf of the South,
I am the black sorceress,
witch of the day and night;
swift powerful, I have driven on till I hate the road,
I with the fire kindled in my belly.

I have raced and outmatched the horse,
my speed flung the sand in the air
and I won, I the black calf.
At the town where the circumcision drum was beating
I came and said I was from where no one knows,
I come from the unknown, from a far-off country.

They asked me what kind of feed I needed
and I answered: none, not like these cowards of yours.
I sleep without food, the all-devourer,
I keep away from the marriage-rites of Ramaesela
for should I enter his enclosure a great cry would rise
like the yell for a leopard among the king's cattle.

At home they say that I am lost –
No pampered child, I am the centipede of the marshes;
hunger does not delay me
nor do I halt from becoming foot-sore,
but the mountains, children of the waste,
demand their price and I pay them.

Not for the sacred spirits do I seek to die,
they who are no man's possession:
but my tribe perish for letting me wander homeless.
I defend the villages from captivity,
brave when the village stands up to danger
and the country says: Where shall I hide them, these cowards?

Ceaselessly on my feet on the iron road
I go falling, falling in the gulleys,
I mimic a river risen in flood
that carries to the mines a man's village.
What can the road owners do to me, the black centipede,
rushing on, fixed to time?

Recorded by H. J. van Zyl. Bantu Studies, Vol xv

S. E. K. MQHAYI

THE BLACK ARMY

Oh yes, we are so thankful
When our homeland gives us a thought
And has us go down to the coast to work
In the hour of its difficulty.
And in any case, who are we
To be able to help the King of England,
The noble gentleman on whom the sun never sets
Who holds his sway over the land and sea
And thinks even of annexing the heavens.

Listen then, young men, you are exalted!
Your nation is in the book of the nations.
You must dance, fellows, line up;
Do this and that, and this and the other!
Do so and so, and so and so on!

When you are set to loading a ship,
On your toes, boys – don't loaf;
The one standing on this side, another over there,
One grabbing here, a second yonder,
Yes men, smart's the word
When you lower the steel cage, man,
Hold it easy with slack arms
And don't stand there all stiff-legged, man,
Lift it up like this,
And shout 'Ho-ha heje-e-e!
Le'm go! Wha – a – a!'

And when you're handling dynamite
Even with fuses and with detonators,
Even electric wires and vitriol
And anything that flames and bursts,
Get hold of it with due care,
Watch your step, keep from harm's way!
But if it happens that a man gets bitten,
Burnt up, nothing's simpler –
Send him to join his fathers
With a solemn service:
Go on like this and that, and this and that!
And so and so and so on!

Go catch the German Kaiser, bring him home,
And cut this war short in a jiffy;
Let the Kaiser come and talk with us,
We'll tell him how the Zulus won at Sandlwana,
Of Thaba Ntsu where the Boers were baffled,
The gathering of wizards at Gwadana.
Be wary when you come to capture him,
You who are used to catch a lion alive.
Do this and that, and this and that!
And this and this and this and that!

Keep that Zeppelin up there in the sky.
When it throws its fires down, hurl up lightnings,
When it scatters poison, throw a powder up!
If it sends electric shocks, use bees!
Confuse it – confusion, confusion, confusion!
Come up on this side and on that!
To bring it down encircle it
Like this and that, and this and this!

They reached their last resort in calling you.
Whatever the disgrace you fall in, leave it there;
And cowardice, don't come back to us with it.
Raise the fame of Africa among the nations
And let your great men be exalted.
They did not simply send you out; you are their pride.
Keep to the law and the accepted rules,
And any new decree, do it like this,
Like this and this, and that and thus!

Off with you then, my fellows, off to France!
Remember the hunger you have left at home.
Sent out to face the slaughter there today,
You're sacrifices for the Black-skinned race.
Go, you bull-calves of the cows with milk-filled udders,
Away, sons of the lean and the long-starved,
And you too, offspring of the death-defiers.
Go, for we have long foreseen all that would come.
Our people's God decided in advance.
Away, your legs uncramped with stiffness,
No quake or tremor in your hearts.
Go with light bodies, limbs unfrightened,
And stride on, stride, stride, stride!
Stand, stand firm, stop, sto-o-o-p!

Mc, C.

THE SINKING OF THE MENDI

Yes, So be it, though we already knew
A long time that this would come, and few
Of were startled for we had seen most
Clearly it would happen as it must.
Out of all ways this was the chosen one –
So then, Lord, your will be done!
And as our bride down her last flood
The Mendi takes the service of our blood.

278

Say it was not for just a bribe
Or for meat you left the hunger of your tribe;
Not in the hope of piling up rewards
Or for wealth counted by the stars.
To you who died for Africa, who sailed down
Over the sea to meet the German, we make it known:
It was not for the King by any loyal tie,
It was not for Britain you went out to die.

When you came from your homes we talked with you;
When you left your children we reached out to you;
Our eyes were wet as we held your hands in ours,
Your fathers groaned, mothers shed bitter tears;
And when you left behind these hills, this earth,
Your backs turned to the rivers of your birth,
Black men of our blood, we said this thing –
'On that far-off field you are our offering.'

With what victim do we make atonement?
For home and family what offering is sent?
Do we not sacrifice the bull-calves of the kraal,
Single out those most loved of all?
So does our way lie open to the heart,
Seeking true words to show the path.
Was not Abel's death the whole world's price?
Was not the Saviour heaven's sacrifice?

Then be comforted, orphans of our nation –
From one death rises new creation;
One man must serve that others may live on.
Accept, and let this pity be your shield;
We say that thus the hurt mind is healed.
And we call old words up from the long past:
'Death is no stranger when it comes at last.'

Ah, those dead stood in the foremost rank
Of Africa – great the ship's burden when she sank.
Brave of the brave they were, men who bring
With their blood greetings to the King of Kings.
Death has its wage – to live again.
Gladly I would stand with them, new-risen men,
And shine like one whose work is well done
In the great brightness of that Day's dawn.
So then, let it be.

Mc., C.

L. T. MANYASE

VUSUMZI'S SONG

This song of mine sets my soul free
Song that brings back my lover to me.
Oh strum the stringed bow for my singing
While I remember the far-off hills
The happy land where no enemy falls.
Sing then as I go lazily swinging!
So says the love-song of Vusumzi.

My heart is far-off between the peaks,
Away off where the South wind speaks,
With her, with the child whom I love,
She who breathes with peace on my spirit,
Who makes lighter my loneliness for it
Till together the piercing days we live.
So says the love-song of Vusumzi.

Remember, my love, the days gone by,
We waited a little with joy, you and I,
I called and you answered and I said, Beloved
Will you hold to your vow, my love, my sister,
The love in your heart never grow less?
Oh beyond the last mountain is my beloved.
So speaks the love-song of Vusumzi.

I shall walk out on the hills but be happy,
And in the dense forest gloom and be happy.
My shield is your only shelter, my love.
I have shed my cares like a thing that's faded
And thrown down my burden unregretted,
And joy springs and I laugh, my love,
To call back again my thoughts of you.

When I go with my love I'm in a small heaven,
And filled with this bliss, a child again,
A little I laugh and my smile undying;
And no sorrow stays long in my heart
No guilt at all nor a nagging thought –
My love is a forest, a bird flying.
So says the love-song of Vusumzi.

You are my lullaby, O my beloved,
And I laugh at the evil days, my love.
Strong in you, strong is my blood
And through me your smile runs a blade.
Your eyes full of love leave me yearning
Beyond all things and the last star shining.
So says the love-song of Vusumzi.

Mc., C.

THE MOTHER CRAB AND HER FAMILY

My children, my little dears,
I'm in a state about your upbringing;
Your older brothers, I have my fears,
Fooled while time went winging.
I could teach and talk to them all day
But never got them to obey.

I've watched your sideways scuttle
Like a lot of crabs, your eyes stick out:
I know that you are stubborn but I'll
Train you yet, I have no doubt.
Aping the older generation
You'll be no credit to the nation.

To begin with then, my dears, walk straight,
Not sideways like the neighbour crab it's
The one thing I really hate,
I'm not allowing such bad habits.
I dislike those who're not like me
Especially among my progeny.

The children tried but gave it up,
They sat down in a row and wept;
Baffled, it made their spirits droop,
So away and in the pool they leapt.
She caught them and with blow and clout
Beat them until they shouted out:

'How do you walk yourself, mama?
We stick to things like a tattoo –
We've only heard you talk so far,
Show us and we'll step like you.
We promise to try the proper amble,
Walk, we will follow your example.'

Sideways she walked, the old mother,
Sideways as well the children learned,
With great respect to one another
Proving the beating was unearned.
So manners win our admiration
And the best manners are imitation.

C., Mc.

ST J. PAGE YAKO

THE YEAR'S ENDING

Now he is gone and we had not understood one another,
The big man left like a flicker of light,
He took up his things and vanished
In the grave of happenings and happenings.
And the beloved friends, the comrades
As well as our beautiful children,
Before it had struck us they were gone too.
With its passing came the youth, the green shoot.
And some have been left weeping,
Yet others rejoice,
Some in the shadow of disgrace
And some free and light.

Difficult enough is the given direction
To keep trust, gazing onwards
And upwards to the clouds
For the promised assistance.
Love your neighbour as yourself –
For as I find myself here at last
The youth who trailed after me has arrived:
Always he has pursued me
And he aimed to seize me in some wasteland
But I fled and left him outstripped like an old man.

I have run the race without wearying
And gazed on steadfastly ahead,
I have not searched guilty and wild this way
And that, and I missed the many pitfalls
That lurk along the trail.
I have run the race that was set for me,
Set by Him, the great Power,
He who was before the being of all things.
For along the road there are snares and catches,
Swift streams and roaring torrents;
Lightning flashes and the earth is torn apart.

But with my gaze still steadfast on the goal
No harm from all these came to me.
Racing, I heard the voices shouting
At me – What is it drives you on?
I fled and I left behind the winds,
Pursuing in the footsteps of my father
Who in the closing year had run his race,
Rested and was refreshed, not to return again,
Never until the uttermost end of time.

Mc., C.

A. Z. NGANI

PRAISES OF KING GEORGE VI

Bull with the fierce eyes that none dares look at,
you are as the colour-flickering water snake,
the fabulous one no man dares stare in the face.
We, the amaXhosa, salute you! We give you a new name.
We raise our voice: Aa, Zanoxolo!
You bring peace to us.
The war is at an end, you it was that finished it;
the enemy is scattered, the nations are tranquil.
Aa Peace-bringer! Aa Zanoxolo!

Storm-sky rolling with thunder,
you thundered over Hitler, severed him body from soul,
his panoply lay in the cold dew,
he fell in an instant, struck into the ground.
Yes, you killed the man with the sullen face.
Hero of London, distinguished in battle.
Yes, in the tidings of mighty events,
in the assault on London by the Germans,
you stumbled but rose again, warding off the blows,
and escaped hard-pressed from the impasse like a man.

Child of the old King, you come
when the great place of the Xhosa is in ruins.
There is no rope to bind on the village thatch,
and we speak, opening old sores.
We remember men who knew power and service to the state
for with us men are chosen who are wise
to make company for kings.

Most beautiful one, handsome when you laugh,
you bend like one at play,
flexible even in war like a reed.
It is well that you have come and harmonious,
Rain-bringer, you come bearing rain,
the rains of Autumn that we may reap fruitfully.
Leave with us this boon – peace, freedom;
share your wisdom with us, your learning, art!

C.

TRADITIONAL

PRAISES OF THE KING TSHAKA

He thinks of war

Son of the righteous one, he who thunders on the ground,
bird, devourer of other birds,
great leaper who bounds over all others –
the hill on whose sides are no grazing cattle,
where the antelopes browse in herds,
the waterbuck feed and the crawling thousand-legs.
Red paradise flycatcher
as if with a head that is dust-covered,
he is making sport of the Swazi king Sobhuza.

He overwhelms the King Zwide

He is the stealthy leopard and for long
he has blocked the river crossings against the rabble,
blocking the way against Ngobe of Zwide's family
who had to go over by the drift at which females cross.
He is the river ford with the slippery stepping-stones
and they slipped on the stones, Zwide and his son.
A wild beast, he rose from the thickets in anger against
     the people.
Storm thundering down on the town of Kugoba,
he bore off the shields of their Amaphela regiment.
The calf mounted to the house of Zwide's mother
while the others said it was madness.

He felled Nomahlanyana born to the king Zwide,
he slaughtered Sikhunyana born to Zwide,
he felled Nqabeni and Mphepha,
He ate up Dayingubo born to Zwide.
Ceaselessly he pursued the man.
I wondered at him chasing the son of Langa
forcing him to the sun's rising
and then following him into the West.

Tshaka takes advice

Old men forever rail against the young,
but I shall listen to the tale of an old woman,
one whom I find alone in the ragged corn gardens.
And I shall hear the tale of an old man
whom I find alone along the trail.

The women mock him

He was the joke of the women of Zululand,
they joked while they sat in his celibate hut
saying that Tshaka never would rule,
that it was not his to be King.
And indeed it was in the year he began to live in
    comfort.

He punishes treachery

Uzihlandhlo and Gcwele are wizards
for they failed to tell Tshaka of the crossing,
showing him instead that which still ran with blood.
The people of Majola were annihilated
and a heap of bones are the children of Tayi
who had lain ready in ambush;
even this day the ridge of Tayi's children stands
    amazed.

He is foiled by Moshesh

The locust was caught in the shaft of the assegais
 among the ancient tribe of Mlandela,
and when it flew up it travelled far.
He scaled up to the heights of Mbozane
and there the dancers for him were a line of grey
 antelopes
and a rooster started up and blocked his way.

Tshaka wearies of killing

The buffalo stands at bay on the great river
and the Pondos tremble to descend on it.
He went out and seized the cattle of Faku in Pondoland;
he seized those of Gambushe in Pondoland;
he took those of the Basuto, the blanketed ones,
and those of the Baca who wear fringed hair.
Ungengi, cease from killing the enemy, it is Summer
and your feet will be entangled in the grass.
Tshaka is not to be spat out, nor is he like water.

His name is fear

I saw the grey hawk swoop like a bolt on the cattle
 of Macingwana,
the blazing fire of Mjokwane's son,
the devastating rush of fire
that burnt out the Buthelezi like owls.
Tshaka! I fear to speak the name Tshaka!
For Tshaka was king of the people of Mashobane.
Raving mad he ravened among the towns
and until dawn came the towns called to each other.
He seized firmly the assegais of his father,
he who was like the maned lion.

BATTLE SONGS OF THE KING TSHAKA

1

Oye, oyeye,
Single out the cowards!
He who rides the lion
Conquered.

2

Let us go out to battle –
Resistance is finished!
From whom did you hear
that resistance is over?
Iyeyi!
From whom did you hear
resistance is at an end?

3

We will go and fire Qolwane's house
we tell no lies, we tell no lies.
You hated us, yes hated!
Oyeyiya wo!
We will go and burn the house of Qolwane.

4

He finished the ruin of the nations,
where can he now wage war?
Hho! hho! Eya ehhe!
He scattered the enemy
he struck the nations.

PRAISES OF THE KING DINGANA (VESI)

He assassinates Tshaka, his half-brother

Vesi, the black one, the leaper who sprang
on the dance-ground of the fighting men
at the place of Death,

subduer of our one where the Elephant grazes,
he bent our great one at Bulawayo.
He is the deep pool which is in the river
that waters the royal town
where a man was drowned as he was washing.
Giver of a helping hand, he stood by
and the man sank with his head-ring and all,
he of the place of Slaughter.

He makes a raid

Black stick of the ancestors of Punga and Mageba
that beat on the waters and stirred up mud,
till out of the muddy water horned cattle emerged.
The red-billed finches in flight collide
high in the air and I cannot tell
which one of them will fall with a broken wing.
The goat of Dambuza who killed the king's lover,
they have seized it by the ear
and quietly it submitted to the blade.

The King has forebodings

Twilight which is the darkness of dawn
the loomings that are shadows below the mountains,
he kept his eyes closed in the shadows of the mountains
and so was like the hunters of the fallen king Mavela.

The beauty of the King

He is hairy as with the mane of a lion
which even on its legs has its hair-tufts.
Umkwamude cut me with a blow on the chin
so they sewed me with an awl and stitched my nose.
The butterfly with broad marks on its wings,
I touched it and there was the frown of anger.
Tree whose trunk is beautiful even in the great drought,
body with no trace of blemish or flaw –
Vesi eats with his bare back exposed
having no need of a bodyguard to screen him.

He massacres Piet Retief

River crossing of the slippery stones
for there slipped on the stones Piet and his son.
He felled Piet among the Boers, he slew Pieter,
he ate up the Boer with the broken teeth
and him whose teeth are sharp,
he felled that one with a stone flintlock gun
and the Boer with the powerful arms.
He slaughtered Jan, son of Stephanus among the Boers
and Jan the son of Seitzman, the short Jan,
the tall Jan and Jan with a gap in his teeth.
He felled Jan Jembroek among the Boers
and him with a mouth like a honeysucker,
the one with a moustache on his lip,
the wing-bender and him who fires a gun with two
     nostrils.

He fears the spirit of Tshaka

The shield of the people of Zwide
remained on the high hill of the Swazis,
there being no man able to take it.
Vesi slaughtered a dancing party of grown girls
among the people of Mashobane.
He is no more said to be a fortress,
they say now that he is a cave of refuge,
for the spirit which is in the house of Mashobane
     is feared.
As he beat about the undergrowth for a leopard
up jumped a hyena.
That hyena was Mxama who buried the king,
and his face at the back of his head is shaped
as are the horns of the buffalo cow,
and others are formed like the face of the she elephant.

He is murdered

He is in a hurry and stir, the deserter of his army,
our bearded one at the place of the Bull Elephant.
The enemies do not stab Dingana
as he advances upon them.
They kept watching the tracks of his feet
thinking to stab him on his return from the march.
And then, at his return
they joined in stabbing frogs in the river.

LOVE-SONG OF THE WATER CARRIERS

I met with the girls coming from afar off,
They carried the pain of lovers in water-jars,
They came to the river pool and poured out the pain.

Desire came to me, the Trouble-maker, and trembled
    inside me.

Trouble-maker, drive me away over the hills
To search for a girl whose heart is all one
For the hearts of these others are double.

LOVE IS BITTER

Age grips the body but the heart stays young,
The wooden bowl wears through with many meals,
No tree-trunk in its age can keep its bark,
No lover rests but that his rival weeps.

NGONI BURIAL SONG

The earth does not ever grow fat
it swallows the head-plumed fighters
and we shall fall to the earth – Nhi hi hi!
The earth does not ever grow fat
it swallows up the swift-acting heroes
and shall we die, we too? – Nhi hi hi!

Listen, Earth! Do you wish to make us mourn?
Listen, Earth! Shall all of us die? – Nhi hi hi!

The earth does not ever grow fat,
it makes an end of the kings
and we shall fall to the earth – Nhi hi hi!
The earth does not ever grow fat,
it swallows as well all the hearts
and shall we die, we too? – Nhi hi hi!

Listen, O you who sleep, wrapped close in the grave,
shall we all go down in the ground? Ho ho ho ho!
Listen, O World! for the sun is setting now,
we all shall enter the earth.

SONG OF THE BUSH-SHRIKE

My father is dead
and I was not told.
My mother is dead
and I was not told.
My heart in pain
cries:
to
toto
totototo.

COME HOME

Song of the Mine Workers

Come let us be going my brothers
Let's make for home.
Come, let us be off
to see the small hills of Tugela.
We worked too long there down the mines
an age ago we left our homes
for this place, this Gold-town.
When we come home they will be waiting
mothers rejoicing as we cross the step
to home, home, my home.
Come brother, let's make for home.
Oh return, leave the Gold-town
leave the uses of the city
caress our children
love our fathers' race
and they'll speak then with handclappings
and happiness as we go in
they'll be waiting there at home.
Come, come home.

c.

LALELA ZULU

Listen Zulus
listen to what the people tell me
about this land of ours.
We hear how the clans are chattering
chattering about you
like so many birds*
and we say birds, we mean the golden finches
they who stripped the cornlands
of Dingana and Senzangakhona.
Ha! they finished them off!

* Birds: A nickname for the whites

B. W. VILAKAZI

BECAUSE

Just because I smile and smile
And happiness is my coat
And my song tuneful and strong
Though you send me down below
Into unbelievable regions
Of the blue rocks of the earth –
You think then I'm a gatepost
Numb to the stab of pain.

Just because of the laugh on my lips
And my eyes lowered in respect,
Pants rolled up above the knees
And my dark hair all dun-coloured
And thick with the roadside dust,
My hands swinging a pick,
And the back stripped out of my shirt –
You think I'm like a stone
And don't know what it is to die.

Because at the fall of dark
When I've unloosened the chains
Of my long day's labour
And I fall in with my brothers
Stamping the ground in a tribal dance,
And we sing songs of old times
That stir up our fighting blood
Driving away all our cares –
For that you think I'm a beast
That breeds its kind and dies.

Because I seem to you a simpleton
Knocked over by plain ignorance
And the laws beyond my understanding
Except maybe that they rob me;
And the house I built for myself
Under the hang of the rock,
A hut of grass for my home
My clothing an empty sack –
You think I'm just an antheap
And not one tear have I in me
To drip out from my own heart
And run over the pure hands
Of the souls who see all.

THEN I'LL BELIEVE

Remembering my father who died in my arms,
10 June 1953, at Umvoti

I'll believe then that you are dead
Only when the crying of birds up in the sky
And night breaking into its bloom of stars,
Small light of dawn still star-sprinkled
That comes through the dark like the moon –
When all these are swallowed and fade away.

I'll believe then that you are dead
Only when the hills and flickering rivers,
The wind roaring from North and South-West,
When the cutting winter frost and the dews
That lay on the grass today and yesterday –
When all these are swallowed and fade away.

Like a star that falls in a far sky
Like wild banana trees clustered along
The sand at ocean's edge, your body fell,
And dreaming I saw you in death's fold
Watching over your face as you grew cold.

A long while the stars were fading, and you,
I saw you weaken and your courage leave:
And for all I knew and all I saw before me
Still I could not in my heart believe.
I'll believe then that you are dead
Only when the sun and the moon both die,
At the time the last clod falls to the earth
And shuddering, all things are fled.

C.

I HEARD THE OLD SONG

At first when I heard the old song
I listened bitter, ignorant,
But now in a new light I make amends.
When your voices murmur in your breasts
Echoing from the depths of old passions,
Carried from the Zulu hills out across the earth,
They call back to me things that are no more,
Faint almost beyond grope of memory
And the long river of my tears.
The song you are chanting, you men of Ngungunyana,
A practised tune for the Vendas of Thobela
Was first sung by the fathers of our fathers
Who dwelt secure in their great homesteads
And through twirling horns of ox and buffalo smoked hemp,
Their women making merry under the trees.
    You strike fire in me, wake me to madness.

ON THE GOLD MINES

Rumble on, machines of the gold mines
Thundering from first light to sun's sinking:
Ah, stop plaguing me, I'll wake up.
Rumble on, machines, and drown out
The groans of the black working men
Whose bodies ache with throbbing weals,
Struck by the thuds of the stifling air,
On their limbs the stink of sweat and dirt:
Sapped of the vigour of their loins.

Call across the distances, old man –
Where you were forged is far away from here,
You were smelted in the furnace blaze
And rising from the ashes you were shipped
So we saw you cross the waters of the sea.
Then a steam train hauled you overland,
Puffing it slid you here at last to Goli.
What a wail you raised, and there came in view
All the rock-rabbits bobbing up beside the line.

Rock-rabbits, yes, of the Black man skinned,
Tailless too, you had them rounded up
Sent them down the pit and bled them white.
Trundle round, iron hoisting wheels,
We don't blame you, you were brought for us
And here imprisoned against your will.
Today you roll on and haul unceasingly,
Though some of you I've seen all rusted up
Pitched out by them onto a rubbish dump.

Here as I pass along the road
I turn around and gazing back
I begin to wonder – what if you bred together
Perhaps, and made increase in swarms. But no!
For these men, your brothers, they rust too
Caught and held fast by the mines.
Their lungs crumble away diseased
They cough, they sink down and they die.
Well, why is it we don't see you cough?

I've heard it said that down the pits
Are nations upon nations of the Blacks,
And men of these tribes raise the white dunes
That make the angry spirits wonder.
There's a story told about the mine machines
That when they shrieked a small black mouse
Peeped out stunned and in a daze;
It was trapped and turned into a mole,
Burrowed in the earth, and so was seen the gleam of gold.

Yes, these burrowers dug underground
And sent up the towering white dumps.
They rooted deep and the ground heaved higher,
Today outtopping the hill of Isandlwana;
I climb up sweeping the sweat out of my eyes,
And here at the crest I watch the dust-coils
Smoke-white that weave and shift
Below my feet, and under shaded eyes
I see how they blot out the world.

Rumble, machines of the gold mines,
Thunder on, clang louder, deeper,
Deafen with such uproar that we go unheard
Though we may groan forever and cry out
And our bodies' joints be gnawed by you.
Hoot your contempt, old machinery,
You have the laugh on us under our burden;
Unmeasured is your power and terrible,
Going your own way as you will, while we obey.

We yielded and came up from our thatched huts
And were herded here together like yoke-oxen;
We left our dark corn and curds and milk
To be fed instead an alien mess of porridge.
Our family pride is gone, we are children,
The world is clearly turned heels over head.
Wakened up at dawn, stood in a row!
Where have you known of a man once buried
Who sees with both eyes open and stands alive?

Thunder, machines of the gold mines
I am awake, not so sick and tottering
And today I am going underground
To drive a jumper drill into the rock.
You too at the pithead, unaware of me,
You'll see how well I work the jack-hammer
Of the white man down below, and watch
The frame trucks and the cocopans come up
Loaded with white rock and the blue ore.

My brother will plod along carrying a pick
A shovel slung over one shoulder,
And his feet cased in iron-shod boots;
He too will go below following me,
The ground takes us burrowers at a gulp.
If I should die down in the deep levels
What matter? Just who am I anyway?
Day after day, you poor sufferer,
The men drop dead, they keel over while I watch.

Such towers were not here to scale
That time I first went underground,
Still I recall the raw deal that I got.
I thought, I'll pack my goods and get home,
But there – ruins and bare fields struck me.
I scratched my head, went into a hut
And asked: Where is my wife, her parents?
They said: The whiteman called them up to work.
Then I was dumb, my mouth sewn up in silence.

Rumble on engines of the gold mines
Even though distant from the location
Your voice that beats sorely against the soul
How it nags and clatters on my ears
Like bronze bells sounding from far off,
It brings thoughts to me of tall chimneys,
Wealth and the wealthy whom I made rich,
Climbing to the rooms of plenty, while I stay
Squeezed of juice like flesh of a dead ox.

Not so loud there, you machines;
Though whitemen may be without pity
Must you too, made of iron, treat me thus?
Hold off your roaring now in those mines
And listen awhile to what we say to you
Just in case we may be unforgiving
On that fine day which is still to come
When we stand up and say: Things of iron
You are slaves to us, the children of the Blacks.

Be careful, though I go unarmed today
There was a time when from these worn-out arms
Long-bladed spears were flung far and wide
Whose whirling dimmed the whole earth;
They shook the empire of the She Elephant*
Thinned out Paul's† boers – then I was struck down.
Now I am forever dreaming, child of iron,
That this earth of my forefathers once again
Will be restored to the rightful Black hands.

But today there's no place to lay myself down
Under the shadow of man's affluence.
The soil of my fathers long has lain fallow
And unploughed, at which I sit and stare.
If ever I raised the hard cash to buy
And claim back the ground my forebears owned
This just right is still denied to me.
God above be witness, and you spirits gone,
Can you bring no end to evils such as these?

*Queen Victoria. †President Kruger.

There in the region of the long-gone dead
Where the countless souls of our race were taken
They say you have an unconquerable power
When you raise up your voice to God
Who disregards the colour of men's skins.
The blood of my veins flows over the earth
Scorched by the sun, clotting and congealed
As I toil on and raise up my prayer to you,
But in reply hear not the smallest sound.

This your fatherland today and yesterday
Is pillaged by the foreign conquerors
Grown rich out of the spoil of nation on nation,
Yet I and this whole line of ours
Who are black are left with nothing of nothing.
We come to the surface and we see the grass
Green to the furthermost rim of sky,
We gaze all about us and call out loud
Wo! But again you do not reply.

Thunder on, engines of the gold mines,
My hands may tremble with the pain,
My feet swell in my boots and stab me,
I have no salve to soothe them for
The whitemen sell their drugs for cash.
Roar on, only stop jarring on my ears,
I have served the white employers well
And now my soul weighs heavily in me.
Run slow, let sleep come to me entranced,
Deep sleep that seals up my eyes
Thinking no longer of tomorrow and the dawn.
Come, release me sleep, to rise far off
Far in the ancient birthplace of my race:
Sleep and dreams from which there is no waking,
Clasped in my vanished people's arms
Under the green hills of the sky.

ACKNOWLEDGEMENTS

For permission to reprint poems in copyright thanks are due to the following:

WILLIAM PLOMER: to the author for poems from *Collected Poems* published by Jonathan Cape Ltd; ALAN PATON: to the author for two poems; HERMAN CHARLES BOSMAN: to Mrs H. R. Lake on behalf of the Estate of the late Herman Charles Bosman; R. N. CURREY: to the author for a poem from *Tiresias and Other Poems* published by Oxford University Press, 1940 and for poems from *This Other Planet* published by Routledge & Kegan Paul Ltd, 1945; MARY MORISON WEBSTER: to the author for six poems; EDWARD VINCENT SWART: to Mrs E. Gluckman and Mr Issy Pinchuck for two poems; DOROTHEA SPEARS: to the author for a poem; ADÈLE NAUDÉ: to the author for five poems; ROBERT DEDERICK to the author for 'Robben Island' which first appeared in *Contrast* and for 'Karoo Town' which first appeared in *New Coin*: F. T. PRINCE: to the author for poems from *The Doors of Stone* published by Rupert Hart-Davies Ltd; JACK COPE: to the author for five poems; TANIA VAN ZYL: to the author for 'The Horses of Marini' copyright Tania van Zyl as it appeared in *Contrast*, 1960 and to Nasionale Boekhandel Beperk for poems from *Shadow and Wall*; ANTHONY DELIUS: to the author for nine poems; GUY BUTLER: to Messrs A. A. Balkema for four poems and to Messrs Abelard-Schuman Ltd for one poem; CHARLES EGLINGTON: to the author and *Oxford Book of South African Verse* (ed. Guy Butler); RUTH MILLER: to the author for poems from *Floating Island* published by Human & Rousseau Ltd (Cape Town), 1965; PHYLLIS HARING: to the author for six poems; DAVID WRIGHT: for a poem from *From South African Broadsheets VIII* reprinted by permission of A. D. Peters & Co. and for poems from *Seven South African Poems* and *Moral Story* published by André Deutsch and reprinted by permission of A. D. Peters & Co.; ANNE WELSH: to the author for five poems; ROY MACNAB: to the author and to St Catherine Press for four poems from *The Man of Grass and Other Poems*; LAURENCE LERNER: to the author for a poem from *Domestic Interior and Other Poems* published by Hutchinson & Co. Ltd and for four poems from *The Directions of Memory* published by Chatto & Windus Ltd, 1964; SYDNEY CLOUTS: to the author for eight poems; D. A. GREIG: to the author for two poems; DOUGLAS LIVINGSTONE: to the author for poems from *Sjambok* published by Oxford University Press; JEAN LIPKIN: to the author for two poems; D. R. BEETON: to the author for one poem; G. C. MILLARD: to the author for one poem; PATRICK ROLAND: to the author and Jack Cope, editor of *Contrast*; PERSEUS ADAMS: to the author for three poems; C. A. FAIR: to the author for 'Chinese Poems: Arthur Waley' which first appeared in *New Coin* (April 1965, Vol. 1, No 2); GEOFFREY HARESNAPE: to the author for one poem; C. J. DRIVER: to the author for three poems; STEPHEN GRAY: to the author for two poems; BARRY O. HIGGS: to the author for five poems; ANTHONY EATON: to the author for one poem; JILL KING: to the author for one poem; EUGÈNE MARAIS: to the Estate of the late Eugène Marais for four poems; C. LOUIS LEIPOLDT: to the Estate of the late C. Louis Leipoldt for two poems; C. M. VAN DEN HEEVER: to the Estate of the late C. M. van den Heever for a poem published by J. L. Van Schaik Ltd; N. P. VAN WYK LOUW: to Human & Rousseau Ltd, for poems from *Tristia* and to Nasionale Boekhandel Beperk for three poems; UYS KRIGE: to the author for five poems; D. J. OPPERMAN: to the author for translations of four poems; ELISABETH EYBERS: to the author for five poems; OLGA KIRSCH: to the author for two poems; S. J. PRETORIUS: to the author for one poem; G. A. WATERMEYER: to the author for one poem; BAREND TOERIEN: to the author for five poems; INGRID JONKER: to the Estate of the late Ingrid Jonker for eight poems; N. M. KHAKETLA: to Oxford University Press for a translation of a poem in *Mantsopa*; E. A. S. LESORO: to the author for one poem; D. C. T. BERENG: to the Morija Sesuto Book Depot for a translation from *Lithothokiso tsa Moshoeshoe*; S. D. R. SUTU: to the Estate of the late S. D. R. Sutu for a poem from *Mathe A Ntsi* published by Oxford University Press (South African Branch); M. A. MOKHOMO: to the author for one poem; L. T. MANYASE: to the author for two poems from *Umlu kaPhalo*; B. W. VILAKAZI: to the Estate of the late B. W. Vilakazi for two poems from *Amal'ezulu* and a poem from *Inkondlo kaZulu* published by the Witwatersrand University Press; ROY CAMPBELL: to the Estate of the late Roy Campbell for thirteen poems; ADAM SMALL: to the author for one poem.

If, through inability to trace the present copyright holders, any copyright material is included for which permission has not been given, apologies are tendered in advance to those concerned.

BIOGRAPHICAL NOTES

PERSEUS ADAMS: Born in Cape Town 1933; educated at the University of Cape Town. Took temporary work as seaman, then stowaway, for which he served in Wormwood Scrubs in 1953. Teacher in Cape Town until 1965 when he left for the Far East to teach in Hong Kong. Returned to South Africa in 1967 and now lives in Capetown. Poems have appeared in literary magazines in South Africa, Britain and the United States and on radio broadcasts. First book of verse, *The Land at my Door*, won first prize in an officially sponsored literary competition in 1963 and was published in Cape Town, 1965.

DOUGLAS RIDLEY BEETON: Born in 1929 at Zeerust in Transvaal; educated in Pretoria and graduated at University of Pretoria and University of South Africa. Qualified and worked as librarian before becoming university teacher. At present Professor of English at University of South Africa. Published verse in *Contrast* and other South African periodicals. Doctoral thesis on novels of George Eliot; radio broadcasts on English poetry in South Africa.

DAVID GRANMER BERENG: Southern Sotho antiquarian and poet. Authority on traditional literature of Lesotho. Published *Lithothokiso tsa Mosheoshoe le tse ling* (1931) the collected praises of Moshesh, in eleven long poems.

HERMAN CHARLES BOSMAN: Born at Kuils River near Cape Town in 1905 and educated in Johannesburg. Taught in Groot Marico district of Western Transvaal, the region of his well known stories collected in *Mafeking Road* (1947). *Cold Stone Jug* (1949) tells of his four-and-a-half years, prison term for culpable homicide. Freelance in Europe for many years. Died in Johannesburg 1951. *Unto Dust* (1963) and *Bosman at his Best* (1965) contained further unpublished stories. Roy Campbell said of him in 1954 '. . . the best short story writer that ever came out of South Africa. His work is full of poetry'.

Guy Butler: Born at Cradock, Cape Province in 1918; educated at Rhodes University, Grahamstown, and Brasenose College, Oxford. Served with S.A. Forces 1940–45. Since 1951 Professor of English at Rhodes University. Former English editor of bilingual quarterly *Standpunte* and more recently editor of poetry broadsheet *New Coin*. His books of verse are *Stranger to Europe* (1952) which includes his war poems, *Cape Coloured Batman*, described by Roy Campbell as 'a masterpiece', *South of the Zambesi* (1966) and *On First Seeing Florence* (1968). Plays include *The Dam* (1953) which won the national Tercentenary Prize, *The Dove Returns* (1956) and *Cape Charade* (1968).

Roy Campbell: Born in Durban 1902; studied at Oxford for one year in 1920 and returned to South Africa. In 1926 he edited with William Plomer in Durban the shortlived but historic monthly, *Voorslag*, (The Whiplash). His *The Flaming Terrapin* had appeared in London two years earlier and he was hailed by Edith Sitwell as a 'poetic tornado'. He left South Africa for good, save for two brief returns, and lived in France, Spain, Portugal and, for shorter periods, in England. Served under the British command in East Africa during the Second World War. Was awarded the Foyle Literary Prize 1951 for his translations of St John of the Cross; Hon D.Litt of the University of Natal 1954. Killed in a car accident near Lisbon 1957. His Collected Poems have been published in three volumes. He translated widely from French, Spanish and Portuguese poets. On his death *The Times* said: 'No poet of the last thirty years has done more original work or compromised less with the current fashions in the literary world.'

Sydney Clouts: Born in Cape Town, 1926; educated at the University of Cape Town. Served in Signals, S.A. Forces in the Second World War. Contributed to anthologies edited by MacNab and Butler, to *Standpunte* and *Contrast* and to other periodicals. Left South Africa 1961 and now lives in London. Anthony Delius said of him, 1959: 'In the latest generation of South African poets . . . Sydney Clouts is outstanding.' His first collection, *One Life*, appeared in 1966 was awarded the Ingrid Jonker Poetry Prize and the Olive Schreiner Poetry Award.

JACK COPE: Born at Mooi River, Natal in 1913; farmed, worked on newspapers in Natal and London. Published verse, *Lyrics and Diatribes* and *Marie* (1948); five novels and two volumes of short stories. Founder and editor of S.A. literary quarterly, *Contrast;* translator with William Plomer of *Selected Poems* by Ingrid Jonker, (1968).

RALPH NIXON CURREY: Born at Mafeking in 1907; educated in the Transvaal, at Bath in England and Oxford. In Royal Artillery during the Second World War and served in the Far East. At present teaches at Colchester, England. His books of verse include *Tiresias* (1940), *This Other Planet* (1945), *Indian Landscape* (1947), translations from Renaissance French poetry and *Between Two Worlds*, a dramatic poem for radio.

SHEILA CUSSONS: A painter, illustrator and poet who has not yet published an individual book of verse; made her debut in *Stiebeuel* (Stirrup) 1946, an anthology of the work of several young and as yet unpublished poets. She lived for many years in Amsterdam and has now made her home in Barcelona.

ROBERT DEDERICK: Born in 1919 in England and educated there; solicitor by profession. Came to Cape Town during war and returned after it to settle. Prizewinner in many literary competitions and was recently awarded first prize in the English section of a national poetry competition; published verse in *Contrast*, *Standpunte*, *New Coin*, etc., and is also well known as writer of light and satirical verse. Lives in Cape Town.

ANTHONY DELIUS: Born Simonstown, Cape in 1916; childhood on a Transvaal farm; educated at Rhodes University, Grahamstown. In South African Intelligence Corps during the Second World War. Worked on newspapers starting in Port Elizabeth in 1947 and afterwards on the *Cape Times*, Cape Town. Lecturer on African affairs at the University of Cape Town. Published verse, *An Unknown Border* (1954), *The Last Division* (a satire) (1958) and *A Corner of the World* (1964). Also published books of prose, including satire, and a play, *Rhodes* (1960). Left South Africa in 1967; now lives in London.

C. J. DRIVER: Born in the Transvaal in 1941, educated at Grahamstown and the University of Cape Town. Edited student periodicals, *Varsity*, *Groote Schuur* and *The Lion and the Impala*. Contributed poems to *Contrast* and other magazines. Chairman of National Union of South African Students. Imprisoned under ninety-day detention law. Studied at Oxford and teaches in England.

ANTHONY EATON: Born in Cape Town in 1943 and educated at the University of Cape Town. First poems published in University magazine *Groote Schuur*, and in *Contrast* 1960. At present teaching in Cape Town.

CHARLES EGLINGTON: Born in Johannesburg in 1918, childhood on a Western Cape farm and educated in Franschhoek and Cape Town and at the University of the Witwatersrand, Johannesburg. Served with the S.A. Forces 1940–45. Newspaper work in Bloemfontein and at present editor of the Johannesburg quarterly, *Optima*. Verse in magazines and anthologies; first volume in process of publication (1968). Art and literary critic, an authority on languages and translator.

ELISABETH EYBERS: Born at Klerksdorp, Transvaal, educated at University of Witwatersrand and lived for much of her productive life in Johannesburg, working as a journalist until 1937. At present she lives in Holland. The first notable woman poet in Afrikaans, her first volume of poems, *Belydenis in die Skemering* (Confession in the Twilight) 1936, has been followed by eight others. She is highly regarded as a pure intuitive poet and her sonnets are considered among the best in the language. A selection of her poems translated by herself and Olga Kirsch into English was published under the title *The Quiet Adventure*.

C. A. FAIR: A nom-de-plume. Born in Kenya and educated at London University. She says of herself: 'I have lived most of my life in Africa and have South African antecedents, though I am not a South African.' After teaching in England and Kenya, she came to South Africa and is now a lecturer in English at a local university. Verse published in *New Coin*.

STEPHEN GRAY: Born in Cape Town, 1941 and educated at

St Andrew's, Grahamstown, and Queens' College, Cambridge, where he edited *Granta* and directed University Shakespearean players. For two years lecturer in English at Aix University now studying at Iowa State University. Poems published in *Voices*, The *Guardian*, *Contrast*, *New Coin*.

DESMOND A. GREIG: Born in Cape Town in 1926 and grew up in Stellenbosch, attending Afrikaans school. After war service as air gunner he returned to Stellenbosch University. Worked as journalist, also magician's assistant in South-west Africa. Published poems and short stories in *Contrast* and other South African periodicals; held two exhibitions of ceramic sculpture. Now edits an art magazine.

GEOFFREY HARESNAPE: Born in Durban, Natal in 1939, and studied at University of Cape Town. Became lecturer in English at Rhodes University, Grahamstown, and is at present lecturer at Witwatersrand University, Johannesburg, where he lives. Short story writer; poems published in *Evergreen Review*, New York, in *New South African Writing*, *New Coin* and other periodicals.

PHYLLIS HARING: Born in Pretoria in 1919. Lived for some time in England and on the Continent and became a regular contributor to magazines, including *Poetry*, Chicago. Her work brought a strong surrealist influence for the first time into South African poetry though her verse has not yet been published in book form. At present a swimming instructor at a Johannesburg school.

BARRY O. HIGGS: Born in Durban in 1943 and matriculated at Glenwood High School 1960. Worked in various jobs as messenger, wrapping parcels, etc. Resumed education at University of Natal until he fled the country in 1964. First poems published in *Contrast* at age of 18.

INGRID JONKER: Born in Douglas in Cape Province in 1933; educated in Cape Town; worked as typist, secretary and publisher's reader. Began writing verse as child and at 16 submitted a first book of poems which was rejected. Published *Ontvlugting* (Escape) a volume of verse in 1956 and *Rook en Oker* (Smoke and Ochre) 1963, establishing her as a brilliant and original poet and winning the country's largest literary prize. Visited Europe briefly 1964 and continued writing striking and often disturbing poems until her death by suicide in July 1965. Posthumous collection of poems, *Kantelson* (Setting Sun) published 1966. Other work includes *The Goat* and other stories, a play, *A Son After my Heart*.

BENNETT MAKALO KHAKETLA: Southern Sotho statesman and poet. Educated as teacher, became editor of newspaper *Mohlabami* (Warrior). Became Minister responsible for Education in the Executive Council of the first Responsible Government of Lesotho, 1960. Member of the Council of the University of Botswana, Lesotho and Swaziland. Author of *Lipshamathe* (poems). Is an authority on the Sotho language and a political adviser to the King of Lesotho.

N. M. KHAKETLA: Southern Sotho poetess. Educated as teacher. Published volume of poems, *Mantsopa*. Wife of the poet-statesman B. Makalo Khaketla.

JILL KING: Born in 1922 in King William's Town, Eastern Cape; educated in Pretoria and at Rhodes University, Grahamstown. Published short stories in South African and overseas periodicals. Poems first published in *New Coin*. She now lives in Cape Town.

OLGA KIRSCH: Born 1924 in the Orange Free State of Jewish parents; studied at Witwatersrand University. Although English-speaking, she was drawn to Afrikaans for her deepest expression. She was a journalist for a period in Johannesburg and now lives in Israel. Two books of verse, *Die Soeklig* (The Searchlight) 1944, and *Mure van die Hart* (Walls of the Heart) 1948; the latter drawing themes from the Bible and Jewish historical sources and containing several striking 'prophetic' poems on race relationships in South Africa.

UYS KRIGE: Born Swellendam, Cape Province in 1910; educated at Stellenbosch University. Lived in France and Spain from 1931–6 learning the Romance languages and writing verse. Journalist in Cape Town 1936; war correspondent with S.A. Forces, captured and escaped from prisoner camp, these experiences forming material of war book *The Way Out* (1946). First book of verse, *Kentering* (Transition) appeared 1935 followed by six others. Krige is also a short story writer in both English and Afrikaans, dramatist, essayist and critic, his work covering twenty-six books, five of which are in English. Through his translations the work of some of the finest contemporary poets in French, Spanish, Italian and Portuguese have been acclimatized in Afrikaans.

C. Louis Leipoldt (1880–1947): Born Worcester, Cape Province; acted as war correspondent for the *Manchester Guardian* during the Anglo-Boer War. Studied medicine in London 1902–7 and after world-wide travels returned to South Africa, working as medical inspector of schools, journalist and, from 1925, child specialist in Cape Town. A fine versatile writer in English as well as Afrikaans, he was one of the 'Triumvirate' of poets who helped rally their people and at the same time clarify and pioneer the new Afrikaans literature. Starting in 1911 with *Oom Gert Vertel* (Oom Gert's Story) seven books of verse by him were published, two posthumously. In the First World War he was physician to General Botha, Prime Minister and Commander-in-Chief. Shortly before the Second World War he wrote a cycle of scathing anti-Nazi poems which have never yet appeared in book form. His most popular book in English was *The Bushveld Doctor* (1937). Described as 'poet, novelist, dramatist, short story and travel writer, historian, linguist, medical doctor of note, botanist, naturalist and gourmet', he was one of South Africa's most gifted men.

Laurence Lerner: Born in Cape Town in 1925; educated at University of Cape Town and Pembroke College, Cambridge. Lecturer in English at University College, Ghana, 1949–53 and at Queen's University, Belfast; now at the University of Sussex, Brighton. Published poems include volumes *Domestic Interior* (1959) and *The Directions of Memory* (1963). He has also published a novel, *The Englishman*, based on the Cape, and essays and criticism.

Ephraim Alfred Shadrach Lesoro: Born 1929 at Platkop, a farm near Ficksburg, Orange Free State, a few miles from the Lesotho frontier. Educated as teacher and now holds a post at school at Gumtree not far from his home. Novelist, playwright and poet, he has published nine books in southern Sotho. Also a freelance journalist, writer of short stories, radio plays and stories for children. His first volume of poems *Mmitsa* (1962) won the S.E.K. Mqhayi prize for African literature. Second book *Mathe-Malodi* has appeared and a third is scheduled. In 1966 he won first prize for poetry in the Southern Sotho section of the national radio competition.

JEAN LIPKIN: Born in Johannesburg in 1926 and educated at Pretoria and Witwatersrand University. Teacher at a nursery school for several years. First poems published in *Jewish Affairs*, Johannesburg and subsequently in literary magazines in Britain, the United States and South Africa. Now lives and writes in London.

DOUGLAS LIVINGSTONE: Born in the United Kingdom in 1932. Served in the Rhodesian police, living for some time at Broken Hill, Zambia. A bacteriologist, he now lives and works in Durban, Natal. His poems first appeared in *Encounter*, *London Magazine*, *Contrast* (Cape Town) and other periodicals. His books of verse are *The Skull in the Mud* (1960) and *Sjambok and other Poems from Africa* (1964).

N. P. VAN WYK LOUW: Born at Sutherland, Cape Province in 1906; educated at University of Cape Town. School teacher and later lecturer at his old University. Main founder of quarterly *Standpunte*, 1945. Awarded Hon. D.Litt. at Utrecht University, Holland in 1948, and two years later became professor at Amsterdam University. Returned to Witwatersrand University as Professor, 1958, and has since remained in Johannesburg. First book of verse *Alleenspraak* (Soliloquy) (1935) followed by seven others until *Tristia* (1962). His *Raka* (1941) is considered the best narrative poem in Afrikaans; he is a versatile essayist and dramatist, best known for verse play *Germanicus* (1956). Louw is widely regarded by critics and fellow writers as the most significant figure in contemporary Afrikaans literature. Hon. D.Litt at Rhodes University 1965; Stellenbosch University 1966.

ROY MACNAB: Born in Durban in 1923; educated at Hilton College, Natal and Jesus College, Oxford. Served with the

Royal Navy in the Second World War; became a journalist in Durban, Natal, and later a cultural attaché in the South African diplomatic service, at present serves in the S.A. Foundation in London. Published verse includes *Testament of a South African* (1947) and *Man of Grass and Other Poems* (1960). He edited *Towards the Sun* (1950) and *Poets in South Africa* (1958), and was co-editor of *Oxford Poetry* (1947) and *South African Poetry* (1948).

ZAKEA D. MANGOAELA: Southern Sotho writer and antiquarian, published 'Hunting Tales' (1913), a collection of 'Praise Songs' of the Basotho chiefs (1921), and was joint author of the grammar of the Sotho language (1927). Teacher and translator of Christian works into Sotho.

LENCHMAN THOZAMILE MANYASE: Xhosa poet, born 1915 at Tsomo, Transkei. After qualifying he began as a teacher at Tsomo Mission and is now at Cicira Training and High School near Umtata. An expert on the Xhosa language, he has written books on orthography and grammar. Volumes of poems include *Imbiza Yesizwe* (The Tribal Pot) and *Umlu kaPhalo* (The Slaughtered ox of Chief Phalo). He is the winner of fifteen first prizes for poetry at bardic competitions in the Transkei and Ciskei since 1959. Other books by him are volumes of essays, plays and a collection of nursery rhymes.

EUGÈNE MARAIS (1871–1936): In the nineties he edited newspapers in Transvaal republic in opposition to Kruger. Left for London to study medicine and law and on outbreak of war joined the Boer cause trying to smuggle arms and medicine through Mozambique. The first literary artist in Afrikaans, his historic poem *Winternag* (Winter night) is regarded as opening an epoch in the literature. His books on nature *The Soul of the White Ant* and *My Friends the Baboons* were published in London and New York and are still well known. Spent the latter years of his life, in addition to writing, as journalist, unofficial country doctor and lawyer until his suicide in 1936. He is a highly regarded short story writer, wrote one play and is still held, despite a small output, to be one of the purest poets in Afrikaans.

GEOFFREY MILLARD: Born at Luderitz, South-west Africa, 1931; educated at Windhoek and Kimberley and at Natal and Rhodes Universities. Taught English to Africans at Fort Hare College 1960–1 and Basutoland University, 1963–6. Studied for the stage for some time. At present teaching in England.

RUTH MILLER: Born in Uitenhage, Cape Province in 1919; educated at St Pius's Convent, Pietersburg, Transvaal. Taught at a Johannesburg girls' high school until 1966. Poems appeared in journals in Britain and the United States and were included in *War Poems of the United Nations* (1943). First book of verse, *Floating Island* was published in Cape Town in 1965 and won the Ingrid Jonker Literary Award for poetry in 1966.

MAKHOKOLOTSO A. MOKHOMO: Southern Sotho poetess. Her first volume of poems, *Sebabatso*, appeared in 1953. *When he spoke to me of love* is an extract from a long poem, *Moratuwa – Lerato la me* (My beloved, my love).

SAMUEL EDWARD KRUNE MQHAYI (1875–1945): Considered the greatest Xhosa poet. Born Tyume Valley, Gqumahashe. Educated at Lovedale College and became active in politics and journalism, nicknamed 'The Poet of our Race'. Edited newspaper *Imvo Zabantsundu*. Lecturer at Lovedale. Wrote two novels, biographies and essays and published three volumes of poetry. Recognized as a famous *imbongi* (reciter of poetry). Adviser to the Education Department of the Cape on Xhosa grammar and usage. His home at Ntab'ozuko (The Hill of Glory) near East London became a national focus.

ADÈLE NAUDÉ: Born da Fonseca Wollheim in Pretoria in 1910. Educated at University of Cape Town and became academic assistant to the University, business secretary, freelance journalist and broadcaster in both English and Afrikaans. Books of verse in English are *Pity the Spring* (1953), *No Longer at Ease* (1956) and *Only a Setting Forth* (1965). Also published a number of children's and travel books.

ALFRED Z. NGANI: Xhosa poet and historian; published *Intlaba mKhosi* (1952) a collection of songs and praise poems of the Xhosa people, and in the same year an historical text book. Lives at Middledrift in the Eastern Cape.

D. J. OPPERMAN: Born in Dundee district, Natal in 1914; educated at University of Natal, becoming teacher, journalist and lecturer at University of Cape Town; at present Professor at University of Stellenbosch. His first volume of verse, *Heilige Beeste* (Sacred Cattle) 1945, was followed by five others, the most notable being *Engel Uit die Klip* (Angel from the Stone) 1950. Has been an editor of *Standpunte* since 1946 and is one of the outstanding Afrikaans critics; editor since 1951 of *Groot Verseboek*, regarded as the most comprehensive anthology of Afrikaans verse. Other works include two plays in verse, the best known being *Periandros van Korinthe* (1954). His achievement in Afrikaans literature is highly placed by leading critics.

ALAN PATON: Born at Pietermaritzburg, Natal in 1903; educated at University of Natal. Taught in Natal schools for eleven years and was principal of Diepkloof Reformatory for non-whites for eight years, resigning in 1948 to become full-time writer. Novels include *Cry the Beloved Country* (1948) and *Too Late the Phalarope* (1953). One of the leaders and chairman of South African Liberal Party until its dissolution in 1968. Hon. Ph.D at Yale 1964. Biography of Hofmeyr, 1964.

WILLIAM PLOMER: Born at Pietersburg, Northern Transvaal in 1903; educated in Johannesburg and England. Farmed in the Eastern Cape, traded in Zululand. First novel, *Turbot Wolfe*, 1925; with Campbell, edited *Voorslag* 1926. Lived in Japan and Greece then settled in England. On naval staff at British Admiralty in the Second World War. Novelist and short story writer; autobiographical books *Double Lives* (1943) and *At Home* (1958) and *Collected Poems* (1960). E. M. Forster wrote of him: 'My favourite contemporary poet . . . Full of colour, feeling, distinction, character-drawing, epigram and mischievousness.'

S. J. PRETORIUS: Born at Postmasburg in the Transvaal and studied at Potchefstroom University. Successively teacher, journalist and broadcaster and at present lecturer at the University of South Africa, Pretoria. He has published six books of verse, starting with *Vonke* (Sparks) (1943). Many of his poems are involved with the Afrikaaner suddenly divorced from his country background and feeling disoriented in the city.

FRANK TEMPLETON PRINCE: Born at Kimberley in 1912; educated at Christian Brothers College, Kimberley; Balliol College, Oxford and Graduate College, Princeton, United States. Served in British Intelligence Corps 1940–46. Since 1946 Reader in English Literature, University of Southampton. Published poetry includes *Poems* (1938), *Soldiers Bathing* (1954) and *The Doors of Stone* (1963), a collected volume.

PATRICK ROLAND: A pen name. Roland has said of himself: ' I farm and run a sawmill in the Eastern Transvaal. Married, have three children, am aged 32. In between all this I write verse.'

DEMETRIUS SEGOOA: Graduate from Botswana, formerly Bechuanaland. His poem, 'Praises of the Train', written while he was still studying was recorded by H. J. van Zyl and published in northern Sotho with a literal translation in *Bantu Studies*, Vol. XV.

F. D. SINCLAIR: Born in Inverness, Scotland in 1921 and came to South Africa when he was on service with the R.A.F. Returned to settle and identified himself with the country; lecturer in English at the University of South Africa, Pretoria. Published verse included *April to March*, *The Nine Altars*, *The Cold Veld* and *Lovers and Hermits*. He was occupied on a book of essays on Afrikaans poets when he died in 1961.

ADAM SMALL: Born at Wellington, Cape Province in 1936; studied at the University of Cape Town and became a lecturer in philosophy at the University College of the Western Cape. His first volume of poems was *Verse van die Liefde* (Love verses) (1957), followed by three further volumes up to 1963. He is also a playwright and essayist.

Much of his verse is written in his own peculiar argot derived from the Cape Coloured population and using a profusion of English and local expressions mixed with Afrikaans. Some poems are wholly in a variety of Cape street English.

DOROTHEA SPEARS: Born in Iowa in the United States educated in Oregon and came to South Africa in her teens; has lived ever since in the Cape. Contributed verse to *Country Life*, London, *Poetry Review, Poetry of Today* and South African and American periodicals. Collections of verse: *Sunshine and Shadows from the South, Van Riebeeck, A Song of Tomorrow* and *No Common Day*. Has also written radio plays and broadcast talks on various subjects.

SAM DUBY SUTU: (full name Sam Duby Raymond Sutu-Mthimkhulu) Southern Sotho poet, educated at Pius XII College, Roma, Lesotho and entered teaching profession, becoming principal of the Moshoeshoe Secondary School at Matatiele in the Transkei where he died in 1965. His historical play *Ho tla na Lebenya Paballong* was published in 1962 and a volume of poems, *Mathe a Ntsi* in 1963.

EDWARD VINCENT SWART: Born in Heilbron, Transvaal in 1911 and was educated at the University of the Witwatersrand, Johannesburg, and Magdalene College, Cambridge, the war interrupting his studies. Became lecturer in English at Witwatersrand; died in Johannesburg 1962. First published poems in Wits University Magazine and in Grigson's *New Verse* from 1936 onwards. Represented in Faber's *New Verse Anthology, The Year's Poetry* 1937 and *Poets of Tomorrow*, Cambridge 1940.

BAREND TOERIEN: Born 1921 in the Porterville district of Cape Province; studied at University of Stellenbosch. Librarian by profession, travelled extensively in Europe and worked at the United Nations, New York, 1949–1967. Now works at University Library, Albany, New York State. Poems first appeared in *Stiebeuel* (Stirrup) 1946, a collection of work by young poets, and his two volumes are *Gedigte* (Poems) 1960, and *39 Gedigte* (39 Poems) 1963, proving his lyrical quality, often ironical, disenchanted.

TOTIUS (J. D. DU TOIT) (1877–1953): Born at Paarl, Cape Province; educated in the Cape and at the Theological Seminary, Burgersdorp, obtaining his doctorate in Amsterdam. He became a minister in the Dutch Reformed Church and later for many years Professor of Theology at Potchefstroom University. With poets Jan Celliers and Louis Leipoldt, was one of the 'Triumvirate' who after the Anglo-Boer War expressed the anguish and suffering of the people in the former Republics. Between 1909 and 1948 published eight volumes of verse; of the three translators of the first Afrikaans Bible (1933) he was the most outstanding, and he is also famed for his rhymed versions of the Psalms.

C. M. VAN DEN HEEVER (1902–57): Born in a British concentration camp at Norvals Pont, Orange Free State. Studied at University of Utrecht, Holland; was a teacher and journalist before becoming a lecturer at Bloemfontein until 1933 when he became Professor of Afrikaans at Witwatersrand. His poetry publication started with *Stemmingsure* (Hours and Moods) 1926 followed by six other volumes. He was principally a novelist, short story writer and essayist, his most successful novel being *Laat Vrugte* (Late Fruit) (1939), and he also wrote a biography of the former Prime Minister, General Hertzog, which appeared in 1943 in both English and Afrikaans.

TANIA VAN ZYL: Born Cape Town in 1908 and studied at University of Cape Town. Lived in Vienna and Paris, studied art and has exhibited paintings and carvings. Her first book of poems was *Window and other poems* (1947) followed by *Shadow and Wall* (1958). Further poems including dramatic pieces appeared in *Contrast*. A third volume, *Rock, Leaf and Grass*, published 1968.

B. W. VILAKAZI: Born at Groutville, Natal, in 1906 and educated at Witwatersrand University, Johannesburg. Lecturer in African Studies at Witwatersrand 1936–47. Poet in Zulu, published *Inkondlo kaZulu* and *Amal' ezulu* volumes of verse. Linguistic authority and joint compiler of the standard Zulu-English Dictionary. The Vilakazi Award for Nguni literature was established at Witwatersrand University in his memory, after his death in 1947.

G. A. WATERMEYER: Born in 1917 at Middelburg in the Cape Province; studied at the University of the O.F.S., Bloemfontein and afterwards moved to Johannesburg where he now lives. His first book, *Sekel en Simbaal* (Sickle and Cymbal) (1947), was an impressive debut, its major theme the nostalgia of the countryman forced into the city. Verse in his two later volumes in Afrikaans is dominated by political and patriotic themes. He has also published a volume of verse in English, *Atlantis* (1954).

MARY MORISON WEBSTER: Born and educated in Edinburgh and emigrated with her family, settling in Johannesburg in 1920. She was 'discovered' by Harold Munro of the Poetry Bookshop, London, and her first book of verse, *Tomorrow*, was published by him as well as *The Silver Flute* and *Alien Guest*. Other poems are *Garland in the Wind* and her selection from all her verse, *Flowers from Four Gardens*. She has also published three novels and is a painter of talent. For many years she has been literary critic of the *Sunday Times* and *Rand Daily Mail*, Johannesburg. In an essay, Uys Krige has said of her: 'She is our finest elegiac poet. . . .'

ANNE WELSH: born in Johannesburg in 1922, educated in Johannesburg and England, graduating at Witwatersrand University and Somerville College, Oxford. Was for some time a lecturer at Witwatersrand University. Poems in various publications including the Oxford *Book of South African Verse* and *Contrast*. Now lives in Johannesburg. First volume, *Set in Brightness* published, 1968.

DAVID WRIGHT: Born in Johannesburg in 1920. Left South Africa in 1934, returning twice in 1936 and 1951. Educated in Northampton School for the Deaf, England, and at Oriel College, Oxford. Lives in London and is active in the literary field and among other work is co-editor of the quarterly review, X. Publications include *Poems* (1949), *Moral Stories* (1954), *The Forsaken Garden* (co-editor) (1953), *Beowulf* (a prose translation) (1957), *Monologue of a Deaf Man* (1958). He also edited the *South African Book of Short Stories* (Faber, 1960). In 1950 he received the Atlantic Award for Literature.

St J. Page Yako: Xhosa poet, has published two volumes of verse, *Umtha Welanga* (Ray of the Sun) 1959, and *Ikwezi* (Poems). He is a teacher at Ayliff, Peddie, Eastern Cape.

INDEX OF FIRST LINES

MORE ABOUT PENGUINS

Penguin Book News, which appears every month, contains details of all the new books issued by Penguins as they are published. From time to time it is supplemented by *Penguins in Print*, which is a complete list of all books published by Penguins which are in print. (There are nearly three thousand of these.)

A specimen copy of *Penguin Book News* will be sent to you free on request, and you can become a subscriber for the price of the postage – 3s. for a year's issues (including the complete lists). Just write to Dept EP, Penguin Books Ltd, Harmondsworth, Middlesex, enclosing a cheque or postal order, and your name will be added to the mailing list.

Some other books published by Penguins are described on the following pages.

Note: *Penguin Book News* and *Penguins in Print* are not available in the U.S.A. or Canada

a volume in the Penguin African Library

MODERN POETRY FROM AFRICA

EDITED BY GERALD MOORE AND ULLI BEIER

This modern poetical geography of Africa is unique. It draws on sixteen countries to present the work of black poets writing in English, French, and Portuguese, although all the poems, many of which appear for the first time here, are presented in English. As a sample of contemporary African writing they reveal an interesting blend of public and personal statements.

Poetry composed in African languages has been left out, because no two editors could possibly have covered the enormous field. This omission, however, does not impair the clear picture of emotional, social and political pressures (fashionably termed *Négritude*) as they are reflected by Africa's imaginative or committed poets today.

This volume has now been completely revised.

AFRICAN WRITING TODAY

EDITED BY EZEKIEL MPHAHLELE

A cross-section (in translation, where necessary) of recent African work in English, French, and Portuguese from the following countries:
Angola, Cameroun, Congo, Dahomey, Gambia, Ghana, Guinea, Ivory Coast, Kenya, Moçambique, Nigeria, Ruanda, Senegal, Sierra Leone, South Africa.

SOUTH AFRICAN WRITING TODAY

EDITED BY NADINE GORDIMER
AND LIONEL ABRAHAMS

This collection of the best recent South African poetry, prose and drama has been made without regard for differences of colour or race and shows the strength of South African writing today. The contributors include Dan Jacobson, Laurence Lerner, Todd Matshikiza, Ezekiel Mphahlele, Lewis Nkosi, Alan Paton, William Plomer and Ronald Segal.

WRITING TODAY

Some reviews of the first four volumes

'Where it seeks to counter the insularities of our taste and the unwillingness, in all but a few places, to study literature comparatively, it is an admirable venture' – George Steiner in the *New Statesman*

'Penguins deserve a resounding cheer for launching this splendid new series of paperbacks devoted to contemporary trends in world writing. If this first quartet is anything to go by, the venture should prove an invaluable introduction to anyone wishing to broaden his literary horizons' – Alan Riddell in the *Daily Telegraph*